QUIT YOUR JOB

QUIT YOUR JOB

OWN A BUSINESS

The Journey From
Employee
to Business Owner

PHIL HOPPER

Quit Your Job by Phil Hopper

1st Edition 2019, pbk.

ISBN: 9781925999112
9781925999129 (epub)
9781925999136 (mobi)

Publishing services by: PublishMyBook.Online

Also available as an ebook from major ebook vendors

This book is dedicated to
Bruce and Jenny Hopper who gave
me the love of reading and learning,
which ultimately gave me the
inspiration to write this book.

Contents

Introduction

To start, thanks for picking up this book to have a read (and hopefully buy? it). I think you have made a great choice, but I am biased. This book is all about the journey and the decisions you will face in making the great leap from being an ordinary employee to owning and running your own business. The book is as much about who should and who shouldn't do this. Quitting your job, abandoning your status as a "salary slave" and taking on the responsibility of owning a business is not for everyone. But, if you have ever contemplated, dreamed or desired to maybe one day own your own business, then this book is for you. If you can stick with me through to the end you will:

- be able to determine if leaving your job and taking on the challenge of owning a business is right for you;
- understand the pros and cons of owning your own business;
- understand what you are getting yourself into;
- have a toolkit to make the journey as easy as possible;
- understand how you can fund owning a business;
- have enjoyed a good read and at the very least, been entertained!

If you haven't already noticed although this is a non-fiction book, I don't intend it to be completely dry. I have written this book more like a conversation that we will be having. I tend to use question marks(?), exclamation marks(!) and the odd bit of **bold** language to ram home what I believe to be important points. If you are allergic to these devices or if you find their overuse offensive, then it might be best to put the book down now!

So why should you listen to what I have to say on the topic? Well I have made the journey from employee to business owner

– twice! Here is a very brief background on my career, if you call it that. My upbringing was fairly standard; my parents were fairly conservative teachers that believed heavily in learning and the academic world. So I had little or no exposure to business or the commercial world aside from being a consumer like everyone else. None of our family owned a business and even family friends were devoid of any entrepreneurs. I went to a decent school, got good results, went on to University (studied Information Technology) and at the end was well educated, well trained and systematised to be a good employee. Whether you realise it or not, the majority of the schooling system and higher education system, all revolves around making you into a productive(?) member of society with all the attributes and behaviours to make a good worker, aka "employee". It is very rare that the schooling and education system teaches anything about how to be an entrepreneur.

After building a reasonable career I started to get the feeling that maybe there was something more to life than just working for someone else. Time and again I would see the fruits of my labour, ideas and effort deliver great results but with minimal payback or benefit to me. Being involved in Information Technology I was up to my armpits in the dot com boom and subsequent crash. At some point, I started to get the entrepreneurial itch. The first foray was my wife and I bought a franchise book store which she went on to run whilst I still worked for an employer. This started the drive and desire but despite having this opportunity in front of me, I didn't take the plunge nor focus full time on the business. After a while we decided to move on from this business (and I will admit this wasn't what you would exactly call a great success; indeed, financial disaster would be more accurate, to say the least).

Finally, I built up the courage to found a Start-up. So I went through the whole process of transitioning from an employee to the owner of a business – a Start-up none the less. This was Journey number 1. I won't go into the details but suffice to say that after our initial capital raising from friends, fools and family, we weren't able to raise more so we ran out of money (in fairness, it was during the GFC and we had an online lending product!). This forced me back into the workforce. Over a few years I made a focused attempt to get back into corporate life and advance my career. After setting a number of goals and 3 different employers, I finally got there as the head of a medium sized technology team in the financial services industry – my core domain knowledge and competency. This was going to be my "forever" job.

Forever and job don't really go together. Within a year or so, the firm was struggling and I was being asked to cut my team. I worked out that I was the person who least wanted to be there – so thus began Journey number 2. I ended up buying an existing business. Before you get too distraught and think, "Why am I reading a book by this loser? All he seems to be able to do is lose money on businesses and ping pong from one job to another?" There is a light at the end of the tunnel. The business that we bought has gone from a "mom and pop" operation to an award winning business and most recently made it into the AFR Fast 100 for one of the fastest growing companies in Australia. Hopefully by the time you are reading this book I will no longer be working in that business on a day to day basis and will be on to my next venture.

I have learned a lot of lessons along the way and half the point of this book it so that you can accelerate your knowledge through my and other's experiences. By reading this, you will understand if moving on from being an employee and becoming a business owner is right for you. It will give you clear and honest truths about what you are getting into and what you can and can't control. It has certainly worked for me.

So enough about me as this book is really about **you** …

If you haven't already, then pull out the credit card – **buy the book** and let me guide you on your journey!

Phil

PART I: The Basics

"The only impossible journey is the one you never begin."
– Tony Robbins

We are going to start the book off at the very beginning! The next few chapters are going to cover the basics of what a business is and help to make sure that we are talking about the same things.

Chapter One
What Do You Mean By "Owning a Business"?

"In the end, all business operations can be reduced to three words: People, Products and Profit".

—Lee Iacocca

Seems pretty self-explanatory, doesn't it? YOU... WANT... TO... OWN... A... BUSINESS! So let's just do it. Not so fast there – if it were that easy and that simple you wouldn't need this book and you would have already done it. At the very least we want to help educate you and give you a greater understanding so that YOU can make the right decisions. Some of that comes down to the basics of what a business really is and what it means to own it.

What do we mean by a business?

Business is a nice broad generic term – the definitions of what is meant by a business isn't as simple as it sounds. Businesses come in all shapes and sizes; they range from your single person enterprise to global corporations employing hundreds of thousands of people. They can also have different purposes and objectives – not-for profit, public companies, state owned enterprises etc. According to the Australian Bureau of Statistics

(ABS) the counts of Australian business as at June 2018 were[1]: (excludes nano businesses with no GST role).

2017-18				
	Operating at start of financial year	**Entries**	**Exits**	**Operating at end of financial year**
Non–employing	1,370,051	259,775	208,717	1,435,547
Employing				
1–4	608,733	85,247	57,606	627,932
5–19	203,351	8,259	11,096	195,619
20–199	52,249	1,136	1,958	50,338
200+	3,915	103	151	3,855
Total employing	868,248	94,745	70,811	877,744
Total	2,238,299	354,520	279,528	2,313,291

If you compare this to the USA, in the most recent census in 2018, they recorded 20,392,068 single-person businesses! There is good news and bad news in these statistics. The bad news is that each year some 70,000+ businesses that employ people no longer exist. The good news is that almost 95,000 businesses (employing people) start each year!

Some of the information below may seem to be a bit focused on the semantics, but it is with a destination in mind. Let me try and simplify it for you. To my mind, when talking about businesses, there are only really two types of business – Small Business and Corporations (i.e. Large Businesses). Then, there are two types

1 ABS 8165.0 – Counts of Australian Businesses, including Entries and Exits, June 2014 to June 2018

of activities that may make you think you are owning your own business – but really are not! These are being Self Employed and being an Investor.

Small Business

The official definition of a Small Business can be very broad. According to the tax man in Australia aka Australian Tax Office (ATO), if you have an ABN (Australian Business Number), you have a business. So you can have no staff, no customers, no income and no expenses and be a "Business". The other end of the extreme, if you talk to a Bank or Financial Institution, they often categorise a "Small" business as one with less than 200 employees and a turnover of less than $50m per annum. That doesn't sound small to me! To refine that a little bit further let's stick with the way the ABS defines businesses:

- Non-employing businesses are sole proprietorships and partnerships without employees;
- Nano businesses are extremely small businesses, have an ABN but no employees and are not registered for GST;
- Micro-businesses are businesses employing between 1 and 4 people including nonemploying businesses;
- Other small businesses are businesses that employ between 5 and 19 employees.

The ATO also defines a small business as one that has a turnover of less than $10m. So we don't bamboozle you with too many conditions and boundaries, the keys to our definition of a Small Business are:

- It has independent ownership;
- The owners have or maintain direct control over operations;
- The owners have contributed most of the capital;
- It has a turnover of up to $10m per annum;

- There is at least one staff member (could be the owner) but probably doesn't have more than 100!
- It sells, distributes or makes a product, or provides services for customers.

Corporation (large business)

Essentially any business that is larger than a small business, we will define as being a corporation. When we "refer" to a business in this book, we are really focussing on the Small Business. Owning a large business has a whole different set of challenges. We are not going to focus on the seismic leap from being an employee to owning a large corporation! We are making an assumption that people would not have the capital or the wherewithal to either create a large corporation or buy one. This doesn't mean that one day your Small Business can't become a Corporation but let's start off small, shall we?

Self-Employed

Fairly self-descriptive – this is where you "surprise, surprise", work for yourself! The key difference here, between this and other small businesses, is that what you are doing is selling your time and services using an independent structure as opposed to being employed directly by another business or organisation. If you are currently self-employed or are thinking of becoming self-employed, please don't feel insulted or belittled by what I am about to say – but being self -employed is not really "owning or running a business". Yes, you will have to undertake a lot of the administrative aspects of owning a business but you are really just an employee, with a bit more flexibility. Where you might have been an employee working for just one firm you now might work for multiple firms. You do get a lot more control over who you work for and when; but essentially, you are still selling your personal time. Examples of this will be free-lance workers, people in the gig economy, you might be a contractor or a consultant. Quite often you will be able to charge a higher hourly rate or provide a fixed price for your services, or sometimes you can even have a recurring revenue stream. In essence you are trading flexibility for price.

There is nothing wrong with being self-employed and many people find that it gives them a sense of freedom and independence, that being directly employed wouldn't give them – BUT it is not a business. Before you get too despondent, being self-employed is often the stepping stone to creating a business. A self-employed person often finds that their services and skills are in high demand and they can't "do all the work themselves" so sooner or later, they hire another person to help and assist and then you start selling their time and efforts. This is really the point in time where you move from being just self-employed to actually owning and running a business.

Particularly if we focus on Australia, there used to be great tax benefits in being self-employed. You were able to buy all sorts of "things" that were supposedly business related and claim them as business assets or obtain outright tax deductions. Governments worldwide are generally cracking down on the "casualisation" of the workforce and the move by individuals and businesses to avoid having employees. The pendulum is now swinging the other way where you are almost penalised for being self-employed – you lose worker protections; there are tax penalties (Professional Services Income taxation) and administrative burdens increase (GST compliance, tax complications, insurance requirements etc).

The key elements here about being Self Employed, your source of income is a result of payments for your time and effort; you are providing services and you are not selling products. So for the purposes of this book, whilst it may be a starting point, it is not the destination – little time or comment will be made about how to Quit your job and become self-employed. Simple outcome – being self-employed is not owning your own business!

Investor

With owning a business – be it a Small Business or a Corporation, a path that you can follow is that of being "just" an investor. This book is focused on those people who are looking at actually getting involved either through management or actively working in the business. So when we talk about "Owning" a business, we are talking not just about an equity stake but taking on responsibility and accountability for the success and outcome of the business. Becoming an Investor in a business is a valid way of accessing the potentially excellent returns available from owning a business.

There are generally two types of Investors – active investors and passive investors. A passive investor is one who treats the investment as just that – a passive investment – it is all about the return that you are looking to get from an investment. The best example of this is buying shares in a listed company. You have no real direct influence or control over day to day activities. An active investor, on the other hand, tries to have influence or some form of control. This is usually obtained via being on the board of directors or conditions placed within the shareholders agreement. It may also be that the other shareholders have sought you out to be an investor, as they may want to tap into your network, knowledge or skills. Assuming that you have the money available being an investor is a great option. You obtain all the monetary benefits that come with ownership – without having to put in the day to day effort. It is not without risk as you have to trust others to have your interests at heart and deliver on their promises. There are many other books out there on investment analysis but we are not exploring this option within this book!

Owning a business

When you own a business there are lots of legal structures under which you can do so. These legal structures are country and sometimes state specific. The key message here is that unless you know what you are doing, get some local and expert advice on the right structure. The choice of which structure you may look to use are mainly driven around a few key factors:

- Limitation of legal liability: this is how you segregate your personal assets and wealth from any cataclysmic downside in your business e.g. lawsuits, debts etc;
- Cost of structure: this is the set-up of expense and ongoing legal and accounting fees to maintain the legal structure of your business;
- Tax implications: the different structures have tax implications for both the (hopefully) profits that you make and also the capital gains tax implications on any future exit or sale;
- Ease of establishment: how easily and quickly you can establish the legal structure;
- Flexibility of ownership: how easy it is to change or alter the ownership of the business.
- Ability to raise capital: if you need access to the capital or funds of others – how easy the legal structure makes this possible.

The basics structures are generally – Sole Proprietor, Partnerships, Private company (aka limited liability company Pty Ltd), Public company or Trusts. The choice of what structure you use will really depend on what you are doing and what is important for you. This is one of those areas where you really should seek independent advice – normally from an accountant!

Categories of business

Ignoring the legal structures there are a few categories of the type of business that you can own.

Start-up Business. Start-up businesses are all the rage -everyone wants to create a Start-up and become the next person riding on a unicorn! What do we mean by a Start-up and why is it different to just creating a new business? Well there are a few characteristics that define a Start-up:

- You are targeting a large market – potentially global
- The business will, conceptually, have the ability to scale up and rapidly
- Exponential growth possibilities
- Requires large amounts of capital to obtain scale and fund early losses prior to a predicted large windfall of cash
- Generally disrupting or creating a new paradigm on a new or existing market
- Has been started with an exit in mind or some liquidity event to make the risk and opportunity worthwhile

To keep it simple we will take the definition as being:

"A startup is a high growth company that is scalable, focused on continually growing, and one where the founders develop an exit strategy that results in either the sale of the company or an IPO" – The Startup playbook – Bharava & Herman.

Whilst still a business, it has some special characteristics. One of the key ones is the need for substantial initial and ongoing capital to achieve the continuous growth.

The reality is that very few Start-ups make it. Statistics abound – but the general consensus is that 9 out of 10 Start-ups fail. 10% you say – sounds like a fair bet – well not so fast. Just because you don't fail doesn't mean you succeed! There are between 320,000 – 350,000 Start-ups commencing each year in the USA. Correspondingly in 2018, there were 190 companies to IPO in the USA with a market cap greater than US$50 million[2]. So if

2 https://www.statista.com/statistics/270290/number-of-ipos-in-the-us-since-1999/

you do the math. 90% fail so 10% survive i.e. about 30,000 per annum given that this is about constant per year. If we assume that every single one of the companies that managed to IPO was a Start-up, that works out at 0.06% (rounded up). So the odds are somewhat against you.

If you look at Australian statistics, there were approximately 250,000 new companies registered in 2017. The majority of these were not "Start-ups" as we have defined them. Over the same year, 115 companies managed to IPO (and that was a busy year – there were only approx. 102 in 2018). You would be hard pressed to identify many of those as being "Start-ups"; maybe 5-10 if you were very generous with your definition! By my count, in 2018 there were 8 Start-ups listing on the ASX.

Whilst a lot of the concepts in this book are equally valid on a personal level for those who want to create a Start-up, the reality is that there are hundreds of books written by people, with a lot more experience (and hopefully more successful) than me, in how to create a Start-up. There are also some very specific needs such as the ability to form a group of successful founders and most importantly raise large amounts of capital; neither of which I will admit I have had much success at. Hence the focus of this book will not be on Start-ups. Sorry. Before you close the book in disgust, I am hoping that you will learn about other opportunities that may be even better for you and also have a much greater chance of personal and financial success. So stick with me and read on!

A New Business. Pretty self-explanatory. A New Business is one that doesn't previously exist that you are going to start from (most likely) nothing! Whilst a Start-up is technically a type of new business, we have put that in its own category. The main difference is that ideally, you will be looking at starting a business that will be healthy and growing will start to generate revenue and become cash flow positive within a short to medium timeframe. It may achieve decent rates of growth but will probably have a limit on how fast it can grow and how far it can scale. It may even be limited geographically. Starting a new business is one of the simplest ways to own your own business.

Most countries make the establishment of a new business relatively easy. Australia has one of the easiest environments to create a new business:

- Create a company
- Create an Australian Business Number (ABN)
- Register a Tax File Number TFN
- Register for Goods and Services Tax (GST)

The above list of activities can be done in about 15 minutes and will cost between $600 if you do it yourself and up to $1500 (including GST) if you engage a lawyer or accountant. If you are paying more than that you are being ripped off. I recommend using www.cleardocs.com.au – they have a simple package that delivers all of the above with the requisite legal documents for $755 + GST (valid at time of writing).

So that is the easy bit. The real difficulty in starting a new business is actually building up a customer base and a brand, to generating revenue. We spoke earlier about the success levels of Start-up businesses. Well the stats on new businesses, in terms of magnitude, are better than Start-ups but still not brilliant.

According to smallbiz trends in the USA, the aggregate of a number of surveys and statistics are as follows:

- A bit less than 40 percent of small businesses fail in the first 4 years.
- In fact, out of all small businesses started in 2014:
    - o 80 percent made it to the second year (2015);

- o 70 percent made it to the third year (2016);
- o 62 percent made it to the fourth year (2017);
- o 56 percent made it to the fifth year (2018)[3]

Other sources of data are pretty similar. The Small Business Association provides another set of statistics:

- o 30% of new businesses fail during the first 2 years of being open (so that means that 70% survive)
- o 50% fail during the first 5 years (so that means that 50% survive)
- o 66% fail during the first 10 years (so that means that 34% survive)
- o And finally that 25% make it to 15 years or more

I may not be an expert on marriage but I believe that you have only a slightly higher chance of your marriage surviving for 15+ years than you do your business. A sobering thought.

The ABS has similarly sobering statistics (not about marriage) for Australia with 60% of small businesses ceasing to operate within the first 3 years.

Whether you look at the data from the USA or Australia, the overall probability is not great. At best you are looking at 50-50 chance of making a new small business a success. You should also note that the above statistics would also include all the Start-up businesses that don't succeed.

If you look at what causes these businesses to fail, the leading reasons for business failure are[4]:

- Incompetence: 46 percent;

---

3 https://smallbiztrends.com/2016/11/startup-statistics-small-business.html
4 https://medium.com/iqvis/4-reasons-why-a-startup-product-launch-can-fail-with-examples-bbd48270f829

- Unbalanced experience or lack of managerial experience: 30 percent;
- Catch all category (includes neglect, fraud, and disaster): 13 percent; and
- Lack of experiences in line of goods or services: 11 percent.

Common new businesses that are started include:

- Restaurants
- Retail trade (frequently franchises)
- Consulting business
- Services – accountancy, book keeping
- Trades – electrician, plumber,
- eCommerce – online sales
- Training – tutoring, fitness,

Recent surveys[5] have highlighted that 4 of the fastest growing small business industries are in:

- Construction
- Home Health Care
- Personal Care Services
- Facilities Services – painting, pest control, moving, cleaning etc

Most new businesses will enter into industries with low barriers to entry i.e. there is not much to prevent new entrants. This is great to get started but not so great to fend off competition. A new business does not need to dominate its market share or even be the only one of its type. It just needs to be able to carve out a niche of sufficient size to generate the returns that is needed.

5 https://www.next-insurance.com/blog/fastest-growing-small-businesses/

A lot of people are inspired to start their own business after having worked in their field of expertise for an employer and are now confident enough in their own capabilities to "go it alone". This is probably the most common way for someone to start a business. They regularly start out as just Self Employed i.e. they are doing virtually the same job, but rather than just being an employee, they "work for themselves". With the right focus, skills and attention this can rapidly evolve into a new business with employees, multiple customers and generating revenue.

Buying an Existing Business. You don't have to start a business to own a business. We have described the failure rate of new businesses and Start-ups above – and as you can see the rate of failure is quite high. That failure rate is also highest in the early years.

- 30% fail in the first 2 years
- 20% more fail in the next 3 years, so a total of 50% fail in the first 5 years
- 16% more fail in the next 5 years
- 9% more fail in the next 5 years

One of the best ways to mitigate this is by buying an existing business. An existing business has managed to sort through a large number of the issues in gaining traction and actually creating a business of some form of substance. Based on the stats above, you should really be targeting businesses that have been around for at least 5 years – ideally 15+ (if you can find them). If a business has been around for a number of years you can see its trading history and hopefully, a pattern of growth or at least, consistent sales i.e. it has a customer base and continues to get patronage from these customers.

You will definitely be paying some form of premium (or goodwill as it is known) for buying an existing business. Occasionally you might get lucky and find a desperate seller – but it is rare that you find a "bargain". If a business is going cheap, there is a good reason for this. Buying an unprofitable business is like trying to catch a falling knife, but there are many people who look for distressed businesses to turn around and reap the rewards. This is not without risk and you will need to know what you are doing.

Looking at decent businesses that have some length of trading history, you would generally look at the follow "cost" to buy a business. Businesses are normally bought on a multiple of EBITDA – Earnings Before Interest Tax Depreciation and Amortisation! Also known as free cash flow.

- Earnings – is simple; that is your profit; then you need to add back the other items
- Interest – this is removed as this is a by-product of how you fund the business. If a business has no debt, it will have no interest payments but one that is heavily indebted, will have a large interest bill. This is removed so that financing considerations are neutralised when looking at the viability of a business.
- Tax – this refers to income tax for the business. This is also removed as there are many ways you can structure a small business to avoid (legally I hope) all sorts of tax payments. Sales taxes etc. should already have been stripped out as part of the revenue and expense calculations.
- Depreciation and Amortisation – this is the writing off of the value of assets held in the business. This is removed as there are too many ways to either manipulate this figure (i.e. increase or decrease write off time frames, leasing equipment, etc.). You do want to take note of the Depreciation Expenses as this can highlight potential problems, where you constantly need additional cash to purchase new pieces of equipment. The actual depreciation expense is a non-cash expense, hence why it is removed.

The purchase price of a business is often expressed as being a multiple of the EBITDA. The multiple of the EBITDA in simple terms, is how many years you would need to own and run the business to recover (in cash) the cost of acquiring the business. The other way of looking at it is, if you divide the purchase price by the EBITDA multiple, you will get the annualised "cash" earnings of the business.

To give you an idea, the rough scale of a multiple of EBITDA for an existing business currently looks as follows:

Business Characteristics	**EBITDA**
Owner operator, limited staff, customers not contracted	2.0 x
Owner operator with some management, customers bound but not necessarily contracted	2.5 x
Operationally sound, regular or positive growth in revenue	3.0 x
Either some form of professional management in place (i.e. not owner, so continuity of management) OR Customers on contracts OR some form of IP in place	3.5x
Manager In place (and continuing in the business) + experienced staff Large market (eg national scope) Customers on contracts Proven sales engine or well known brand i.e. business continues to generate sales without owner's input IP or solid barriers to entry	4.0 x +

Ultimately the price a business is sold at, comes down to what the buyer is willing to pay for and what the seller is willing to sell at. The current market conditions and education of the market is such that the above reflects where the market is at.

When a business is for sale, you need to look carefully at what the seller is "adding" back into their earnings. This is generally done to remove one off items and/or personal expenses that are sitting in the business. Examples will be "business" trips that have been paid for by the business or personal cars, telephones, rent, etc. This is often done by an existing owner to minimise the tax they pay – some of it is legitimate, some can be a bit questionable. A favourite seems to be getting your website developed or paying for some advertising "that didn't work" – look carefully at these and don't hesitate to discuss with any seller the validity of these addbacks. Be very cautious about a business that makes little or no tax profit but make a large EBITDA after add backs. The other area that is a traditional "gotcha" is "owner's salaries" – these are normally added back so that you can see the underlying earnings "to an owner". This is valid but you need to check that it isn't the owner and others – as any working family member will need to be replaced with a salaried employee or the new owners will need additional family members to work in the business.

Franchises. A franchise is really a sub-section on the previous two categories, of either a new business or buying an existing business. So what is a franchise? According to the Franchise Council of Australia:

"Franchising is not a business itself, but a way of doing business. It is essentially a marketing concept"

If those words don't ring warning bells, then I don't know what will. I am a bit biased against franchising as I see the cost/benefit firmly in the Franchisor's camp. People are attracted to franchises as they give a sense of comfort that you are part of a larger group, they provide training and you have an established set of processes and procedures (i.e. a system) backed by a well-known brand. Essentially you are buying into scale.

There are different types of franchises:

- Job Franchise e.g. Jim's Mowing
- Product Franchise (distribution) – local rights to a business/ brand e.g. car dealership
- Business Format Franchise – get the rights to use the brand and full systems and processes e.g. McDonalds
- Investment Franchise e.g. Hotels
- Conversion Franchises – a looser coupling of organisation to obtain brand scale e.g. real estate agents

To make a franchise a valuable proposition for you, it needs to be worth the cost. This makes for a simple equation. So for a franchise to be successful, the franchise that you buy into must give you more in terms of:

FRANCHISE VALUE

- The additional revenue the Brand generates
- Processes and systems cost you less to run/less to develop
- Group buying power reduces costs

EXCEEDS

- the additional costs of Franchise license
- ongoing Franchise Fee
- and any Advertising levees etc.

On top of this, you need to understand that even if you win out on the first point, how much do you have to give back if you build the "asset" that is your business and eventually sell it and what do you actually own? Most franchises are in essence, 5 year licenses to run the business. I would not want to pay very much for the right to a business for just 5 years. So whilst they feel like they reduce your risk in owning a business with the support of an organisation behind you, in reality, franchising as a system works because the Franchisee accepts a lower rate of return than the Franchisor. Otherwise, why would they not just employ people to run their outlets?

Ultimately if you decide to get in to a Franchise, make sure that you do it with your eyes open, since those who have been able to make great returns on franchises have generally, either:

- Bought a Product Franchise or bought a master franchise license for territory
- Ended up owning multiple franchises
- Got in early when the cost of the particular franchise was lower

One of the other contradictions of the Franchise model is that the Franchisor is most valuable to you when you are starting out and don't know what you are doing BUT you are most valuable to the Franchisor when you know what you are doing and you don't need them...

If you go back to the quote from Franchising Council of Australia... "it is essentially a marketing concept"...what that boils down to is that you are buying into a Brand. A franchise can work if the value of the Brand in the marketplace is greater than the additional costs and constraints of the Franchising model.

Despite my negative view on Franchises, there are heck of a lot of them and they continue to prove popular.

According to a Griffith University study, Franchising Australia 2016 revealed:

- There are 1,120 business format franchisors in Australia in 2016, compared with 1,160 in 2014.
- There are an estimated 79,000 units operating in business format franchises, reflecting no net increase in the sector over the past two years.

- More than 470,000 people are employed directly in business format franchises. (So they employ a lot of people, at an average of 6 per Franchisee)
- Sales turnover for the entire franchising sector was estimated at $146 billion. (We are talking a serious amount of business here – run the numbers and the Sales per Franchisee is over $1.8m)
- Sales turnover for business format franchises was estimated at $66.5 billion.
- Only 1.8 percent of franchisees were involved in a substantial dispute with a franchisor in the past twelve months. (So that means more than 1,400 franchisees were in a "formal" dispute with their franchisor – sounds like a lot to me!)

I hope by now you have picked up my bias against Franchising – this is based on both personal experience and dealing with lots of franchisees and franchisors. Most of this bias does come from the Business Format Franchise opportunities. There are fundamental flaws in the business model. I wouldn't recommend buying either a new or existing franchise but it may still be the right path for you. Be careful that you are not just buying a job and essentially becoming Self Employed, where you are exchanging an Employer for a Franchisor!

Not for Profit. At first glance it might seem odd to have a category in here about a Not for Profit business but the reality is that, a lot of the key concepts that we will be looking at, apply equally to a Not for Profit business as any other.

Firstly, to understand what we mean by a "not for profit" – it is essentially a business that has as its primary goal something other than for the purpose of making money for its owners. There are legal definitions (highly dependent on local regulations). According to the ABS, a "not for profit" has the following characteristics:

- They are organisations
- They are not for profit and non-profit distributing
- They are not part of the government
- They are self-governing
- And are non-compulsory!

They contribute significantly to the overall economy both in terms of economic output, employment and contribution to society. The catch and their relevance to this book is that you can't really "own" a not for profit – they are essentially "owned" by the public. You can still start or create one but you can't buy one. Legal structures exist under which you can create one and once again, you are best advised to seek specialist advice on what is the best structure to create for a not for profit.

Secondly, whilst the purpose of a non for profit is for some other reason aside from "profit", the reality is that when looking to have a sustainable not for profit business, you must generate some form of profit. You need to be able to create a business model that provides a mechanism that you can generate enough revenue to cover the costs of running the business. To further drive this point home, if you can't generate enough revenue to exceed your costs then you will not be able to grow and increase the reach of the not for profit enterprise. So in the end, you still need to be "profitable". It is just that the profits are invested further into the business to achieve its outcomes and objectives.

A key consideration when taking on this challenge is having a true understanding of your ultimate objectives – and also ensuring that your passion for this outcome is going to be able to sustain you through all the challenges that you will face. So when reading the rest of this book, whilst I won't refer directly to a not for profit business, the concepts will all still apply.

Chapter Summary/Key Takeaways

Hopefully that chapter wasn't too much for you, with loads of statistics and terms. The key takeaways:

- When we talk about Owning a business, we are referring to real businesses and not just job alternatives (i.e. self-employed workers) or plain investment
- There are lots of different legal structures that you own a business through – please seek some financial/legal advice for the best one that is suitable for you
- The different categories of business that you can own are:
    - o Start-ups (not a key focus of this book – sorry)
    - o New Business
    - o An existing Business that you buy
    - o Franchises

In the next chapter, you will learn what it is really like to own a business.

Chapter Two
What is Involved in Owning a Business?

"People want to start their own business or become financially independent. But you don't end up a successful entrepreneur unless you find a way to love the risk, the uncertainty, the repeated failures, and working insane hours on something you have no idea whether will be successful or not".

—Mark Manson – Self Help entrepreneur.

This chapter will take you through what it is really like to own a business. I will try and dispel some of the myths and give you a realistic view of what you are getting yourself into.

The lifestyle of the business owner

Before we get any further, I want to make sure that if there is only one thing you get out of this book is the crystal clear understanding that owning and running a small business is HARD work. There are no ifs or buts. If the primary motivation of owning a business is to do less work, then by all means enjoy the rest of this book but don't get into owning a business if you are not prepared to put in the hours.

When you are a small business owner, you are wholly and solely accountable. To give you a bit of an idea about what you might need to do to survive – let alone succeed – read on!

Business owner Boot Camp

If you think that you have what it takes to be a business owner here is a suggested boot camp to try out for yourself. This will give you a bit of a feel for what you are up for.

With this boot camp, it is best done ***BEFORE*** you own a business – it will get you fit and ready for what you are up against. If you get through the end of it and still want to proceed, then you definitely have what it takes. This boot camp assumes that you are still working, still have some form of income i.e. you have a job.

The whole boot camp takes 42 days i.e. 6 weeks. It starts on a Monday and there is a Day 0 pre-work. IF you are serious about doing this, I suggest that aside from the Day 0 task, don't read the rest of the boot camp, as it works best if you don't know what is coming!

(There is a Boot Camp checklist at the end of the book that you can photocopy or print out to make the boot camp easier to do.).

You will notice that some days of the book camp are the same as previous ones. Don't panic it is all part of the plan.

Day 0: Before you start, treat yourself to some of the good things in life that you and/or your family enjoy. This could be an excellent meal out, complete with baby sitters for the kids OR go the whole hog and have a luxurious weekend away. This is to develop a memory of what life was or could be like before you own a business.

For best effect we suggest that Day 1 is a Monday.

Day 1: Find a set of paperwork that is probably both annoying, time consuming and somewhat confusing. A suggested example is filling out a previous years' tax return. If you normally have an accountant do this for you, then this is perfect. Try and fill out the return just by looking up online what you need to do. Don't ask others for help. Gather all the correct forms and fill it in. You may not be able to get this done in one setting. But the key here is that it should be done after your day or work has been completed. Record how many hours or days it takes you to do this. If you are an accountant and filling out a personal tax return is easy, fun and a piece of cake, then try something else like linking your medicare, superannuation, any government grants and your MyHealth record on the MyGov website. The main focus here is to do something that you haven't done before that is interacting with the government after hours.

Day 2: Take note of your bank account balance and your credit card limits. You need to go **cold turkey**. For the next 6 weeks you need to survive on just enough to allow you to eat. When we say eat, we are talking a "baked beans" style diet. To give you an idea, you need to be budgeting on say $10 a day plus another $5 per extra person in the household. The way to do this is to calculate the amount you will need over the 6 weeks e.g. if you have a partner and two kids it is $10 + 3 x $5 = $25 per day – so 42 days @ $25 per day = $1050. Take your credit card and withdraw up to the limit in cash. Put the $1050 in your wallet and deposit the rest back into your bank account. Put any other credit cards locked away in a drawer. No eating out. No going out to events (unless they are free). Just bunker down and survive for the 6 weeks on the allotted amount.

The following are to be done in conjunction with the baked beans diet.

Day 2: Whatever your usual form of transport to get to work, use another means. If you drive – get public transport. If you get public transport – take another form (or drive). You should still try your best to get to work on time.

Day 3: No special tasks – just eat your baked beans and survive.

Day 4: Another day of baked beans (or your chosen incredibly cheap form of food).

Day 5: Before you leave work for the day, leave your keys or access card on your desk (ideally in a place that can't be stolen).

Day 6: Make a trip to your workplace. If you recall you do not have your keys or access card – so you will need to find some way to be able to get inside the workplace and retrieve your keys or access card.

Day 7: Make a trip to your workplace. Grab a bunch of documents – it can be emails printed out. Take them home and read them. Hang on to these documents.

Day 8: Get to work an hour earlier than you normally do. If you were unable to retrieve your access/keys on the Sunday, you will need to work this out.

Day 9, 10, 11, 12: Work through lunch. Do not eat lunch. Make sure you still hydrate yourself by drinking water.

Day 13: Have a day off. You have earned it.

Day 14: If you still have the documents from Day 7. Place them in a bag or some form of box. Ideally give this container or box to one of your family members. Ask them to select a document and write a special number on it (they can make it up). Get them to hide the container somewhere dry and that doesn't require a ladder to reach it.

Day 15: Look up the rules on NSW payroll tax and determine via reading case studies, under what conditions an owner driver contractor would make you liable for NSW Payroll tax.

Day 16: After finishing work at around 7pm, once you get home flick the switch off on the circuit board where you live and survive until the next morning without power.

Day 17: Find out from the facilities team at your place of work what day of the week the cleaners come to clean the office.

Day 18: Leave your mobile phone at home when you go to work. IF your work demands that you must have your phone to do your job, then after arriving at work, go back home and get it. Otherwise survive the rest of the working day without it.

Day 19, 20: Work through lunch. Do not eat lunch. Make sure you still hydrate yourself by drinking water.

Day 21: Spend the morning trying to find the container of documents from Day 14. Once found – find the piece of paper with the special number on it and confirm the number with the family member.

Day 22,23,24,25,26: Work through lunch. Do not eat lunch. Make sure you still hydrate yourself by drinking water.

On the day of the week that the cleaners come in to clean the office, you will work back until the cleaners arrive. You only need to do this for one day of the week. On that day you can have lunch BUT you need to remain in the office (ideally doing work). Between your normal work finish time and until the cleaners arrive, you cannot contact your family. If they call multiple times, send them a text to say that you are ok but will be home later – something urgent has come up at work. (If you have nothing better to do whilst you wait at work then I suggest reading a book – ideally this one).

Day 29: On this evening have a family member set an alarm between the hours of midnight and 5am. When this alarm goes off, get up – throw some clothes on and drive to your nearest 7-11 or all night service station and buy a random snack. You can eat it– but remember to stay within your Baked Bean diet budget!

Day 30: Cut up your credit cards(s). You are probably getting tempted to have a splurge and eat a decent meal by now.

Day 31: Whatever your usual form of transport to get to work – use another means. If you drive – get public transport. If you get public transport – take another form (or drive). You should still try your best to get to work on time.

Day 32: Cancel your credit cards by contacting your financial institutions and request replacement cards. After doing this, work out and make a list of all the regular direct debits and charges that normally hit your cards.

Day 33: Before you leave work for the day, leave your keys or access card on your desk (ideally in a place that can't be stolen).

Day 34: Make a trip to your workplace. If you recall you do not have your keys or access card – so you will need to find some way to be able to get inside the workplace and retrieve your keys or access card.

Day 35: Make a trip to your workplace. Grab a bunch of documents – can be emails printed out. Take them home and read them.

Day 36 – 40: Repeat the same set of activities that you undertook for Day 22 through to 26. This time let your family know that on the night of the cleaners, you will be home late.

On the night of the cleaners – make good use of the time and update all your details that require your new credit card numbers. If you don't yet have the new card(s) then perform this task when you have them. It is likely to be some time this week.

Day 41: Try and walk all the way from you home to work ie don't use any public transport or car.

Day 42: Congratulations you have finished business owner boot camp. Find any of your other hidden credit cards, put them back in the wallet. If you have any cash left over (highly unlikely), then I suggest that you take what is left of your family out and thank them for their patience. A big gift of some sort is in order for your partner to apologise for the last 6 weeks. Hopefully you have saved some money during this time. Have a look at your bank account and see how much more is in there. This number is very, very important as it shows you how much you can save or survive on when Armageddon happens. (Oh and I suggest that you pay off the credit card – particularly the cash withdrawal, as this will be accruing an usurious amount of interest.)

Just out of interest you should weigh yourself and you will probably find that you have lost weight. We are not suggesting the small business owners boot camp become a new diet fad!

Boot Camp debrief

If you are planning on doing the Boot Camp then you can still read this section. There are some spoilers but not enough to ruin your... fun!

After going through the actions they may seem a bit frivolous and silly but I can guarantee you that nearly every small business owner has been there and done that. The scenarios that I have had to deal with over many years don't even make it onto the boot camp list. Just to help you understand why going through it and the tasks are necessary – here are the lessons that you can takeaway:

Cashflow: This is the *lifeblood* of any small business. More businesses go out of business from the lack of cashflow than anything else. There will be some time during your life while running a business, where through (possibly) no fault of your own, the cash in the business will dry up. This can be due to adverse trading conditions, an unexpected large bill – normally from the tax man, etc?. Sometimes you can even run out of cash due to the success of the business. Whilst there are lots of financing options to deal with this, there will surely come a time when for whatever reason you are just going to have to tighten your belt and survive on minimal cashflow. Having a small taste of this (and your family as well), will give you some insight and at least allow you to plan for it or know what works and what doesn't.

Dealing with the unexpected: I can't tell you what may or may not happen when you are running a business. What I can tell you is that as the owner, the buck stops with you. If something goes wrong or needs to get done you can't always rely upon your staff to do it. There are times when you will need to do things from the sublime to the ridiculous. You just do. If you can't handle things coming from left field and having to "deal with it" then you had best partner up with someone who can. A business doesn't respect birthdays, weekends, anniversaries, etc. It will throw up curve balls when you least want or expect it to.

Endurance and sacrifice: The reason the boot camp goes for 6 weeks is that to be a successful owner of a business you don't just have to perform for a few days, but you need to be in it for the long haul. Throughout this time, you will have to make sacrifices not once, but many times. It may be as simple as working through lunch through to giving up weekends after weekends.

It doesn't just impact you: Whether you are married, have kids or just young and single, what happens with owning a business doesn't just impact you. With the sacrifices you will need to make to be a successful business owner, it has an impact on others around you. The boot camp is as much about getting your family and friends exposed to "losing you" to your business, just as much as it is to give you real insights as to what you are up against.

Annoying sh*t: At some stage during owning a business – probably monthly (maybe quarterly, if you are lucky) – you will need to suddenly become an expert in something you know nothing about. More often than not, this will be a piece of local, state or federal government legislation. Hopefully you will have access to some advisors but sometimes you can't afford or even they don't know – you just need to work it out. The internet is a great resource but with access to vast amounts of information comes vast amounts of confusion!

There are lots of aspects that the Boot Camp did not deal with – it mainly looks at the personal impact to you. It doesn't cover two key items that you are likely to lose more sleep over than anything else – staff and customers. Maybe at some stage I can add in components to the boot camp to approximate some of these challenges. (Feel free to email suggestions and ideas.)

Chapter Summary/Key Takeaways

To own your own business is definitely hard work. As the owner, the buck stops with you. If something goes wrong and no one else can fix it then YOU are the fixer! A business can absorb as much time as you give it and will take and steal time when you are not looking. It is not for the faint hearted or lazy. It is not a path to instant riches. When owning your own business, you will face many challenges:

- Cashflow
- Dealing with the unexpected
- A test of your stamina and endurance – both mentally and physically
- Impacts to family and friends

Despite all these challenges, every year, hundreds of thousands of people either start up new businesses or set out to own their own business.

We now need to understand why YOU want to own your own business.

PART II: Motivation

An American investment banker was taking a much-needed vacation in a small coastal Mexican village when a small boat with just one fisherman docked. The boat had several large, fresh fish in it.

The investment banker was impressed by the quality of the fish and asked the Mexican how long it took to catch them. The Mexican replied, "Only a little while." The banker then asked why he didn't stay out longer and catch more fish?

The Mexican fisherman replied he had enough to support his family's immediate needs.

The American then asked "But what do you do with the rest of your time?"

The Mexican fisherman replied, "I sleep late, fish a little, play with my children, take siesta with my wife, stroll into the village each evening where I sip wine and play guitar with my amigos: I have a full and busy life, señor."

The investment banker scoffed, "I am an Ivy League MBA, and I could help you. You could spend more time fishing and with the proceeds buy a bigger boat, and with the proceeds from the bigger boat you could buy several boats until eventually you would have a whole fleet of fishing boats. Instead of selling your catch to the middleman you could sell directly to the processor, eventually opening your own cannery. You could control the product, processing and distribution."

Then he added, "Of course, you would need to leave this small coastal fishing village and move to Mexico City where you would run your growing enterprise."

The Mexican fisherman asked, "But señor, how long will this all take?"

To which the American replied, "15-20 years."

"But what then?" asked the Mexican.

The American laughed and said, "That's the best part. When the time is right you would announce an IPO and sell your company stock to the public and become very rich. You could make millions."

"Millions, señor? Then what?"

To which the investment banker replied, "Then you would retire. You could move to a small coastal fishing village where you would sleep late, fish a little, play with your kids, take siesta with your wife, stroll to the village in the evenings where you could sip wine and play your guitar with your amigos."

—Anonymous parable found on the internet

Chapter Three

Why do *You* Want to Own a Business?

So this is where we start to get real and personal. Owning a business means different things to different people. Whilst I haven't done a scientifically executed survey of thousands of potential business owners, I have a pretty good handle on many of the reasons why – having been there and done it myself (a couple of times). Here are some common reasons:

- To be in control of your own destiny
- The lifestyle
- Work life balance, spend more time with the family
- Flexibility
- Have a passion for a line of work
- Work location
- Don't want to work for someone else
- Personal satisfaction and self fulfillment
- Oh and of course… the money

A survey conducted by smallbiztrends in the USA as to the main reasons why people started a business – came up with the following[6]:

6 https://smallbiztrends.com/2019/03/startup-statistics-small-business.html

- Ready to be his/her own boss: 26 percent;
- Wanted to pursue his/her passion: 23 percent;
- The opportunity presented itself: 19 percent;
- Dissatisfied with corporate life: 12 percent;
- Laid off or outsourced: 6 percent;
- Not ready to retire: 6 percent;
- Other: 5 percent;
- Life event such as divorce, death, etc.: 3 percent.

Before we go any further, grab a pen and paper or create a word document on your computer, phone, ipad, laptop, etc (in future I will just call these your "Device") and list down **why** you want to own a business. This doesn't have to be a grand earth shattering mission statement that will inspire a generation of workers – just a simple list of what is driving you to want to own a business.

This list is useful to come back to and don't be frightened to change it as your thoughts and desires change as well. You are not anchored into this. What I would suggest is that you look at the list again then order these in terms of priority i.e. what is most important to you. There is nothing wrong with a short list of only 2-3 items or a list that is 20 items long. But the longer the list, the more important it is that you prioritise the order.

We are going to call this list your **Motivation List**. Keep it safe, don't lose it – we will come back to this again and again later. Add, subtract, reorder – whenever you have a better understanding of your motivations – but **keep** this list and make sure it is **written down**!

Now look back over your Motivation List and try to identify the "emotive" reasons. These are normally highly subjective (nothing wrong with that) but it helps if you drill down to what it is you actually want. Here are some examples:

- **I hate my boss**: whilst this is probably true (and it probably goes both ways as well), you have to get passed this and understand why this is driving you to want to own a business. The underlying reason is more likely that you don't want to work for someone else i.e. you want to be in charge or have a greater degree of autonomy.
- **I hate my job**: once again most likely true – but why do you hate your job – is it the pay, is it the long hours, is it the location?
- **I want to be like (insert name in here):** you may know someone that owns their own business and you wish to either have the same sort of success, wealth, social status as they do. You need to drill down on this and understand what it is about them that you really want – is it the money? Is it their good looks and charm (owning a business won't make you more attractive – indeed it may go the other way)?

I am sure that there are many reasons that I haven't listed above but the key is to list them down. Try and be factual and outcome focused rather than emotional. And put them in priority order! We will now look at some of the most common reasons and look a bit closer at them.

- Control
- Lifestyle
- Self fulfillment
- Financial

Control

So you want to be the "Boss"? You may not be a complete control freak but chances are, you like the idea of being in charge or in "control" and calling the shots. Owning a business can give you this level of "power" or control. Self-determination is a great thing. The flip side to this is that you have to be prepared to make decisions in a timely and sensible manner. The buck stops with you.

Assuming you own a business you will, by defacto, be in control. So a powerful aspect of owning your own business is definitely having control. This allows you to set the scene and dictate what, when, how, etc. This is very much a big plus in owning your own business. I am sure that we have all had that moment at work – where you have just had to do something that you thought was neither right, sensible, enjoyable, logical, etc. and you have just had to do it. The larger an organisation, the more likely this will occur.

With control, you can also influence the next item on the list Lifestyle. By being the boss, it enables you to have control over flexibility. This may be around working hours, location, strategic direction, etc. Control gives **you** flexibility. For some, the control aspect is more about what you don't want to do rather than what you want to do.

So what happens if you don't want control or it is not an important driver for you? Well depending on the size of the business, you can always delegate control to others. This can also be very empowering for those involved. As the owner, you still maintain ultimate control; but on a day to day basis, others can still call the shots. Sometimes being in charge is not what people really want. The added stress and accountability around making decisions can be worse than the alternative, which is allowing others to take control. Issues around control do not have to dominate the daily activities of the business – indeed aspects of control only generally come up when either big decisions need to be made or something goes wrong. A business with a good and well communicated plan – that has the engagement and buy in employees – will have little or no issues around control.

One tip – even though as a business owner you are in "Control", there are still an enormous number of aspects that you can't dictate and control. Three items that you will probably do more than just struggle to influence are:

- Staff
- Customers
- The Government (at various levels)

So if control is very important to you, there needs to be an acceptance that there are items that you can't control. If you are on the "control freak" level of the spectrum – developing a coping mechanism will be important for your stress levels and long term satisfaction. So understand that control will never be absolute, but the level of control when you own your own business is much, much greater.

So, should you get into business with others? Well if control is important to you, entering into owning a business with others may become problematic for you and so you would need to carefully consider this option. The better scenario may be for you to only consider having passive investors (i.e. people who provide financial support but let you run the business on a day to day level). Alternatively, you probably want to get into business with others where control is not as important to them i.e. via formal arrangements, it is agreed that you are in "control". This would normally end up with YOU being the CEO or Managing Director or just the Manager i.e. the Boss.

Lifestyle

Normally when people talk about lifestyle in conjunction with owning their own business, they are thinking about things like:

- Work life balance
- Being able to spend time with family

- Flexibility with work hours
- Flexibility with work location aka working from home

So I hate to burst your bubble but if by "lifestyle", you mean doing less hours and spending more time with your family and friends, then you are gravely mistaken.

"Scottish Pacific's SME Growth Index, which has surveyed more than 1200 small Australian businesses, found more than 40 per cent of business owners say they work between 60 and 80 hours (a week)."

Just absorb that statistic – more than 40% of owners work, what I describe as, bullsh*t hours. For a five day working week, even at 60 hours a week, that is 12 hours a day – doesn't even include the time to travel to work! Even if you spread this over 6 days, you are talking about 10 hours a day. Note that this statistic does not talk about the owners who work *more* than 80 hours a week.

Don't kid yourself – owning a business is hard, time consuming work.

Any fanciful notions that you have about spending more time with your family – forget about it. Unless your family is with you on the journey and actively working in the business, you won't get to spend more time with them. But wait you say, "I know many small business owners that have a great work life balance". This is true, you probably do. But I can almost guarantee you that they spend a whole heap of time on the business that you never seem to hear or know about – late nights pouring over tax returns or bank accounts, worrying about where all the money has gone. They have also probably spent many years prior, doing excessive hours of work.

There is a light at the end of the tunnel. Once you have been running a business and got it operating successfully, there is much greater chance that, should you choose to do so, you can spend less time on it. Small businesses do NOT run themselves no matter what someone else tells you. They require a firm hand on the tiller at all times – letting that go and leaving it alone is a recipe for disaster. Whether you buy a business or build one from scratch, you need to prepare yourself for at least 5 years of intensely time consuming, hard work.

You may, depending on the business, have some level of control and flexibility about when you work. The key point being, that the volume of "when" will still be very high! One of the good aspects with a lot of small businesses is that you have a high degree of flexibility about where you run the business from. There will also be elements where you may be working 80 hours a week, but 40 of these you may be able to do from the comfort of your own home! Unless you have a retail business – with the capabilities of modern technology or an online style of businesses – this is a real opportunity if location is important to you. Please note that often, part of the niche of the business that you operate in will be your location. This can be a critical factor in attracting customers.

Let me repeat that – you need to brace yourself ***for at least 3-5 years of the hardest work of your life,*** if you are to be successful. You can certainly run a business by only spending a capped amount of time – but the probability of success will be low. Hard work alone won't guarantee success but it will improve the odds dramatically. If you recall previous discussions about franchise businesses, one of the reason the franchise model "works" is that the franchisee will put in more hours and effort than a normal employee would i.e. accept a lower rate of return!

If lifestyle is the burning reason that you want to own a business, then unless that lifestyle is one of being a workaholic, you will be bitterly disappointed. You may obtain some flexibility in the timing of the hours – but not the sheer volume. You will also have some flexibility on the location of the operations (and where you do your work from). These are important considerations as to how this fits into your lifestyle.

Self Fulfillment

A big driver for many business owners, is Self Fulfillment. What do I mean by that?

- Doing something that you are passionate about
- Being driven by success
- Setting goals and objectives and achieving them
- Building something that you own, that is yours
- Being the beneficiary of your hard work and effort
- Doing something for your family

If you are lucky, you may be able to own a business in a field that you are truly passionate about. You may be passionate about the environment and start an eco-friendly resort, recycling business, sell eco-friendly goods, etc. You may be passionate about cars and start a racing car business, sell specialised after-market goods, import rare cars etc. Having something that you are passionate about will help you on your journey. If you are sitting there putting in 80 hours a week, you would hope that it is something that you like doing! Being able to combine a passion and owning a business can only assist you towards success.

It is not all about just being passionate about what you do. If I draw upon my own experiences in owning a business – my business was intimately involved in the motor vehicle industry – if I am honest, I don't even like cars and would prefer to take public transport! Despite this, I would note that I found it be the most self-fulfilling experience of my life. What do I mean by that?

Back when I was working for an organisation, I had the benefit in most instances of being fairly committed (one might go so far as to say "passionate") about the places and the work that I was doing. Being dedicated and putting in long hours was not an issue for me. For the most part, I was engaged and enthusiastic about my work. Owning your own business takes this up a gear. Even though I never lacked the motivation, it is different when it is your own business. Have you ever faced these scenarios?

- You have delivered something of substance e.g. landed a new client, delivered a big project, provided outstanding customer service BUT you feel as though you have not quite received the accolades or compensation for it?
- You have worked hard for little or no thanks
- Provided day in, day out service
- Have ideas that you would like to put in practice but are unable to, either from lack of interest from the organisation or lack of financial support
- Had someone take the credit for something that you have done
- Built a team or a business… but someone else is reaping the (financial) benefits

When you own your own business anything good that happens in a business is… **yours**. You can choose to share this with others but you, as an owner, are **the** beneficiary of everything good that happens.

- A client says thanks for providing great service. That is a Thank You – direct to **you**.
- A new client comes on board. That is **your** new client
- Win a piece of new business. That is **your** bottom line that gets bigger.
- The business grows by 10%. That is **your** business asset that is growing.

- There is a great team of people working in the business. That is **your** team.
- Every time a customer pays for a product or service. That is them paying **you**.
- Every time you pay a staff member their regular pay. That is **you** helping them to make a living.
- The business is successful. That is **your** success!

If you are ever motivationally challenged, then owning your own business is great way to charge up your motivation levels. If it can't get you moving, probably nothing will. Knowing that what you (and the rest of the team) are doing will directly benefit you makes a huge difference in what you do. This is one of the key reasons why small businesses can succeed where big business struggles. A business owner has that extra level of care and passion around the result; will go that extra level to ensure a customer is happy, if not, delighted with the result.

Financial

"It's not about the money, money, money ..."
—Jessie J, Price Tag 2011

Yeah right! I suspect that pretty close to the top of the list for most people in why they want to own a business are the financial rewards – Money. It won't be the only reason and for some, it will not be a major consideration but odds on, it is fairly important.

So let's get real. For the majority of people, it is easier and less risky and more financial rewarding to have a job! When you factor in the hours of work and the risk of failure and possible loss of capital, the short term returns for owning your own business are not great!

A study by Fundera[7] in the USA showed that small business owners work harder but don't make as much as the traditional CEOs. 86.3% of them take less than $100,000 a year. To compare, the average salary of a traditional CEO is $163,000. More surprisingly, the study revealed that 30.07% of the small business owners don't even take a salary. Most business owners say they pay themselves between $20,000 to $50,000 per year! Ouch!

For most, a job offers a regular pay cheque, some form of contribution towards your retirement and a fixed and relatively known quantity of hours to work. Owning your own business won't necessarily give you any of the above!

One of the hardest aspects about going from being an employee to owning your own business will be the change in the way you will earn money. Unless you are purchasing an existing business, there is likely to be a long lead time between earning the same amount of money as you used to earn as an employee. This is one of the reasons why people often take the first step of becoming Self Employed before moving into owning a business.

Let's say that you have decided to start your own business – you will probably need a certain amount of capital upfront to get it started, buy equipment, fitout an office or shopfront. Then you will need to open your doors and will likely have sales/marketing/advertising expenses upfront. Aside from the initial cash drain, the more important aspect is that by and large, it will take time to start generating revenue and profits. Customers will need to become aware of your services, location – you will need to build a brand and reputation. This process can take years. During this time, it is highly likely that your business will not be generating the desired returns that you are seeking.

---

7 https://99firms.com/blog/small-business-statistics/

If the pay is less, the hours are greater and the risks much higher – why are people financially attracted to owning a business?

You are building an asset that you own.

When you own and grow a business, every $ of profit not only provides a direct return to you, but it starts the process of building your asset – your business. This is how it works. Let's say in the first year of running your business you manage to generate a profit of $50k. Well done, that is $50k more than last year. You would have received the $50k in profit or you may have re-invested this back in the business. If you remember this table, we brought up when looking at buying a business:

Business Characteristics	EBITDA
Owner operator, limited staff, customers not contracted	2.0 x
Owner operator with some management, customers bound	2.5 x
Operationally sound, regular or ongoing positive growth in revenue	3.0 x
Professional management in place, Customers on contracts	3.5x
Manager in place (and continuing in the business) + experienced staff	4.0 x +

So not only do you have a business that has "paid" you $50k, but the business is now an asset that on the open market could conceptually be worth $100k! Suddenly $50k has turned into $150k. Let's take this further. You work really hard and grow the business by say 20% – once again, well done. This takes your annual profits to $60k. But the asset value of your business is 2 x $60k so $120k – so the $10k increase in profits translates to $10k in profits and another $20k in asset appreciation. Taking it even further, you continue working hard (you will note that "hard work" is a recurring theme) and after say, 4 years you have a business with a few employees and it makes $100k per annum – on top of that you now have 4 years of a growth story and some people who can do the work for you. Your business is generating you $100k of earnings per annum (nice), but more importantly you now have a real asset. As it now has more substance and a decent operational history, you have moved from a 2x multiple to 3x multiple! The asset is now 3 x $100k i.e. $300k.

This is the financial payoff for being a business owner – the creation of an asset, both from a self-satisfaction perspective and also a financial one. The key here is that the financial payoff can be substantial BUT it is not a path to quick wealth. It is the ultimate **accumulation strategy**.

Chapter Summary/Key Takeaways

Hopefully this chapter will have prompted some thought about why you want to own a business. If you haven't already got the message, you need to understand that owning a business requires long hours and lots of hard work. For at least the first few years, it is not conducive to a sensible work life balance.

You should have your prioritised Motivation List of what is important to you when thinking about owning a business. Major categories of motivations are:

- Control – yes, you can be in control of your own business
- Lifestyle – will be that of a workaholic!
- Self fulfillment – a successful business can be very fulfilling
- Financial – short term pain for longer term gain

If I haven't scared you off already, in the next chapter we will explore if owning a business is right for you!

Chapter Four
Is Owning a Business Right For *You*?

"The only place where success comes before work is in the dictionary."
—Vidal Sassoon

You have your Motivation List, you are aware of how much work and effort owning a business can be – so it is really right for you? What we are going to do in this chapter is compare the relative strength, weaknesses, pros and cons for the sliding scale of opportunities out there. I have tried to present this in a summarised format for ease of understanding and viewing. It is somewhat subjective so if you don't agree with the viewpoint put forward, feel free to have your own interpretation. Also, there are no absolutes so I have had to generalise. For example, when you are an employee, your autonomy level is generally low,– however, there are some workplaces and managers who allow a huge level of autonomy. Ultimately as an employee, you are only given as much autonomy as the employer allows.

A few quick notes about the table below:

- When talking about a business, we are really talking about a Small Business. I have not split out Start-ups or whether or not you are starting from scratch or buying a business. The attributes below are not really impacted by those details.
- I have split out Joint Business Owner, Business Owner (assumes 100% or you have only passive investors) and Franchise. The reason these are separated, as you will see from the table below, is that they have a big impact on two key criteria – **control** and **risk**.

- Control and Autonomy sound like the same thing, but in this instance, control refers to the business i.e. you determine what the business does. Autonomy relates to you and how you can dictate what it is that you do.
- Access to funding refers to both your ability to get funding via standard channels i.e. borrowing from a bank for either business purposes or personal use e.g. obtaining a Home Loan.

Employment Type / Factor	Employee	Self Employed	Joint Business Owner	Business Owner	Franchisee	Investor
Control	Low	Medium	High	Very High	Medium	Low
Autonomy	Low	Medium	High	Very High	Medium	Very High
Flexibility	Low	High	Medium	High	Medium	Low
Location	Low	Medium	High	Very High	Medium	N/A
Termination of employment	4 weeks notice	Job to Job	Share-holders agreement	Nil	5 year Franchise Agreement	N/A
Job Security	Low	Very Low	High	High	Medium	N/A
Ability to Quit/Exit	High	High	Low	Low	Low	Medium
Work life balance	Varies but mostly High	Varies but mostly High	Low	Low	Low	High
Work Hours	Low	Varies	High	Very High	Very High	Nil
Self fulfillment	Low	Medium	High	High	High	Low
Rewarded for success	Varies but mostly Low	Medium	High	Very High	High	Medium
Regular Income	Yes	Not guaranteed	No	No	No	Usually
Building an Asset	Nil	Nil	High	Very High	Medium	Low
Wealth Creation	Nil	Low	High	Very High	Medium	Medium
Tax Effective	Nil	Low	Medium	High	High	Medium
Access to funding	High	Medium	Low	Low	Medium	Nil
Complexity	Low	Medium	Very High	High	Medium	Low
Risk	Low	Medium	Medium	High	High	Medium

Going through the table above hopefully makes it clear what you are actually getting yourself into. There are lots of common misconceptions:

- Being an employee confers a high degree of job security. You just have to look at what happens during an economic downturn – jobs are not secure. Most employees have, at best, 4 weeks notice to be terminated. High level managers and the like often have "golden handshakes" and long "gardening leave" clauses but for the average worker, these don't exist.
- Self-employed is running a business. Well not really. Yes, it has some legal aspects that are similar to running a business – indeed you may be self-employed under a limited liability company but if what you are selling is you and you alone, then really you have a casual job or contract employment. This does not mean it is not a comfortable stepping stone to running a business, but more about that later.
- Franchises are a safe way to own a business. As mentioned previously, whilst a franchise potentially provides you a lot of training and "support" services, in practice it is not risk free. You have all the risk present in owning a normal business, plus the risk of losing your Franchise or not having it renewed. You also severely limit your upside re Wealth Creation and building up an asset. Most Franchise agreements have the franchisee taking 25-50% of the gain in value of any franchise on the sale of the business.
- Owning your own business is a recipe for work life balance. Business owners working in their business are probably the hardest working "employees". A small business can consume an unlimited amount of time. Hopefully it gives back in value over the longer term but this is not guaranteed.
- Owning your own business gives you flexibility. In owning your own business, you do have "control" over what you end

up doing. This gives you day to day flexibility; however, there are limits to this. You still need to run a business and that may involve doing a lot of things you don't want to do. In addition to this, a small unlisted business is very illiquid – meaning your ability to leave or sell out is very hard. It can take years to exit from owning a business, particularly if you want to maximise the value you want to get from it.

Criteria for a Successful (small) Business Owner

On one side it is important to understand what it is that you seek (want); the other side is that you need to understand what criteria or skills you need to have to make it as a successful Business Owner.

The first step in being a successful Business Owner is to not have your business fail. If we look at reasons that small businesses fail (not necessarily Start-ups or large corporations), the music stops when either you are unable to pay your debts or you run out of money. These are normally symptoms but not the root cause. The internet is awash with articles on why businesses fail. If you combine these, you will find the following:

- Lack of or poor business planning
- Starting a business for the wrong reason
- Cashflow management
- Poor Management or leadership
- Too much or underestimating competition
- Market Fit / Lack of differentiation
- Expanding too quickly

When you look through this list the majority are about decisions. Only one really comes to your personal level of skill and that is, poor management or leadership. The great news about that is that it is easy to learn and there are lots of courses to help with people management and leadership skills.

So what then are the criteria to be a successful Business Owner? These are far more about your attitude and outlook than anything else. The keys are:

- Motivation and hard work
- A willingness to learn new skills and accept training and tutoring from others
- Understanding what you are good at and what you are not. For those aspects that are important to the business e.g. good cashflow management you either need to employ people to do this or outsource e.g. to an accountant or others.

There will definitely be skills that you will need to learn and acquire but running a business isn't rocket science. Despite this, it will certainly help if you have had a background and experience in the following:

- Accounting and Financial management
- Selling
- Customer Service
- Human Resource management
- Business Development
- Information Technology
- Marketing
- Logistics and Operations
- Legal & Contracts
- Specific domain knowledge of the industry the business operates in ...

If the above seems like a list of subjects from a business degree or an MBA, you would not be too far wrong. All of the above can be learned and more importantly – outsourced! Decide what it is that you have in terms of skills and capabilities and find ways to make up for any short falls. Whether you are a master of one or a jack of all trades – it doesn't matter. What is important is understanding what you are and having a plan or idea as to how you will make up for the others. You will be surprised at what you can pick up and learn; you may find out that you have talents that you never knew existed. If you did have to pick a "skill" that you should have, it is a willingness to learn new things because as a business owner, there are always new things to learn!

Chapter Summary/Key Takeaways

Before you embark upon owning a business, you need to make sure the outcomes that you are after, align with the realities of owning a business. It may not be for you. Alternatively, you may be licking your lips with anticipation at the prospect.

Businesses demand a wide and varied skill set. It is unlikely that you will be proficient in all of these skills. That is what employees, consultants and outsource firms are for. You need to be more concerned about the attitude and outlook that you take into owning a business:

- Desire to work hard
- Willingness to learn new skills
- An honest view of what you are not good at and preparedness to seek help!

In the next chapter we will look into how to start the journey...

PART III: The Journey

Chapter Five
Have You Got a Plan?

"By failing to prepare, you are preparing to fail."
—Benjamin Franklin

Or the paraphrased version of it – by failing to plan, you are planning to fail!

Plan, what Plan? Absolutely, you need to have a plan. You have got your prioritised Motivations List of why you want to own a business. You should also have a view as to whether or not you really want to own a business – and if so how you would prefer to structure it. I am assuming that if you are still reading, that you are still keen on the idea (or if not, you are at least learning something). Let's start planning.

Just to make it clear this is a plan as to how you are going to Own a business; it is not the plan for the business.

Creating the plan

At this point in time I should point out that my background and forte is in project planning. This is exactly what you are about to undertake, a Project. For simplicity, let's call it project OMOB – Own My Own Business. If you can't come up with a fancy acronym don't let it stop you but by giving something a name, you breathe a little bit of life into it and make it real.

So step one – give it a name: Project OMOB

I am not going to lecture you on how to do project planning (lots of other books for that, might try and pen one later... depending on the sales of this book). For simplicity, I am going to take a task oriented approach to the plan. There will be four main elements that we will focus on:

- The scope – what it is you are going to do
- The schedule – a fancy name for the list of tasks and the timeline
- The resources – stuff you need to execute the plan, including people and money
- The risks – things that will bugger up the plan – and how to avoid them

There are other aspects and elements to project planning but as I said, we are keeping it nice and simple. When looking at tasks within this plan you need to think of everything in terms of:

- What – the outcome or objective or task
- How Much – what is the quantitative outcome of the task
- When – pretty straightforward; by when does it need to get done by (this may be aspirational or a real deadline)
- Who – you won't need to think about this because chances are, 9 out of 10 tasks are going to be done by, well, YOU!

To get this moving you will need to decide where you are going to document and run this from. Pros will reach for some fancy tool like Microsoft Project Plan but a simple excel spreadsheet can work wonders or for those who live in the cloud, Trello is a nice simple product.

Scope

This is the most important part of the plan. This is where you work out what the end objective is and what is actually going to get done. If you don't know this then the rest of the plan will struggle to be worked out.

The good news is that, whilst you should feel free to change this, the scope is fairly straight forward. Here is an example scope (you need to document this):

Objective: To leave my job and own a business by [insert date here]

The profile of **My** Business will be:

- Bought/ Started from scratch
- Located at:
- In the field of:
- Have a Return on Investment of:
- A target Revenue/ Profit (EBITDA) of: within [x] years
- Needing $ [xxx,xxx] to fund the business
- With an exit planned for [x] years or once [y] result has been achieved
- Owned via the legal entity of:
- To help me achieve my goals of: [Financial Independence/ Save the world/ Make Money/ Build an Asset for my Family/ Create a lifestyle of/ Self Determination/ Self Fulfillment]
- Any other criteria appropriate to your desired business: [online only, no staff, doesn't operate on weekends (good luck!), environmentally friendly, not for profit, Not in industry XYZ, can expand globally, scaleable, growth prospects, cashflow generator etc]

Other standard tasks that you will need to complete as part of the scope of works:

- Undertake an assessment of your strengths and weaknesses
- Develop a list of training or experience that you need to acquire
- Undertake an assessment of your current financial assets
- Research the industry/ business that you intend to Own
- Engage/ find a Lawyer/Conveyancer, Accountant, Financier, Business Coach (if required).

Schedule

Based on the scope above you will list out the tasks that you need to get done. As stated previously think of each task as an outcome. The *What, How Much* and by *When*. We know the *Who*, it's you! The tasks are what you actually do i.e. an outcome. To give an example if a task is to "undertake an assessment of your strengths and weaknesses", you would be better structuring it as follows:

ID	What	How Much	When	Who
21	Get feedback from work colleague as to Strengths and Weaknesses	3 Colleagues	2nd Feb	Me
22	Produce list of Strengths and Weaknesses	1 Document	7th Feb	Me

Another item that you need to consider when producing the schedule/ timeline, is what tasks *depend* on others i.e. what do you need to do first? In the above example, you need to get the feedback from work colleagues before you produce the list!

The key thing with the schedule at this stage is that you need to a) write it down, don't just leave it in your head; b) be realistic with your timeframes. After you have created the whole Schedule you may need to re-assess the overall timeframe objective.

As you work the plan, you need a mechanism to track your progress. Tasks should be marked as complete once done. Keep it simple – a task is either complete or it is not. There is no value in a task that is 90% done. It is amazing how the last 10% seems to take as long as the previous 90%! If something is too complex, then you can always break it down into smaller tasks.

The key thing with the schedule, is that it is there to drive you to your outcome in the time frames that you want. There is no point writing it then not using it to drive your activities!

Resources

At this stage resources are generally limited i.e. you don't need that many. The types of resources generally required will be:

- Money
- People
- Equipment
- Software/Licences

You may require some funds to pay for either equipment, training, software/tools. So it is good to work out what you might need here. You may also need to allow for some travel if you are undertaking some investigation.

People are important and part of your initial plan will be to find appropriate consultants/ service providers that can help you on your journey. Ideally you should NOT have to pay them anything at this stage.

The key with the resources is understanding what resources you need and working out how you will acquire/ pay for these. The resources required should link back to your schedule in terms of Who is doing What.

Risks

Risk management is an important part of any plan – and indeed running any business. Risk management is not easy but you don't have to get too caught up on it. The purpose of Risk management is getting you to think ahead of what could go wrong and what are you going to do about it. When looking at a risk, you analyse them in 2 ways:

- Impact: If this risk was to occur, what would the impact to the project be?
- Likelihood: What are the chances that this will happen?

The combination of the Impact and Likelihood will determine the priority you need to place on the risk. A left field example would be like the Risk of a volcanic eruption – the *Impact* would be huge – but unless you live, say, on Hawaii, the *Likelihood* is very very low.

Once you have worked out the priority of the risks, there are only really 3 strategies to deal with risks:

- Accept: this means that you roll the dice and hope it doesn't happen
- Mitigate: you take activities to reduce either the impact or the likelihood
- Avoid: this effectively means taking our insurance so that if it does happen you are compensated for the cost

What are the likely risks that you will face? The biggest risk is actually YOU! For Project OMOB the main thing that can stop it, is you. This is likely to occur when you are losing your resolve or not being focused on the outcome. Some other potential risks are:

Risk	Likelihood	Impact	Action/ Strategy
Key person leaves project/unavailable (YOU)	Low	High	Accept
Unable to obtain funding	Medium	Medium	Mitigate
Unable to find an appropriate business	Medium	High	Mitigate (expand criteria/ allow more time)
Unable to obtain resources	Low	Low	Avoid

Just like the schedule, you need to monitor your risks – add to it if more come into play and take the necessary actions. Risk management is not a passive activity, it is an active one.

As a small business owner you always need to be thinking of the risks not only to your project but also ongoing for your business. Whilst it is not likely to be a big issue for Project OMOB, the skills and practice you get from doing this will serve you well when it comes time to run your business!

Chapter Summary/Key Takeaways

You need a plan to Own your own business. This chapter has given you a simple framework to create that plan. A plan is as simple as:

- Scope
- Schedule
- Resources
- Risk Management

A plan is only useful if after you write it, you then work that plan and execute it. The plan is the moment whereby you bring together all of your thoughts from the previous chapters and pull it together. You are really going to make this happen!

The following chapters are going to drill down on how to execute the critical elements of that plan!

"A good plan today is better than a perfect plan tomorrow".
—George S Patton

Chapter Six

What Business do I want to own?

"I'd rather be a failure at something I love than successful at something I hate."

—George Burns

Big question – so what business do I really want to own? Previously you have pulled together a prioritised Motivation List of why you wanted to Own a business (Chapter 3 in case you have forgotten). If you haven't done this, then I suggest you do it now otherwise this next section is going to be really hard and probably futile!

When we went through the reasons of Why, we never delved into the What or the How. This is very important as sometimes you will have too many preconceived notions. For example, you may say that you really want to own a restaurant, but is that compatible with your life goals? If a life goal is to be able to spend time with your family, unless you run a café that only opens at lunchtimes and doesn't open on weekends then it probably isn't going to happen (and probably wouldn't be a highly successful business either).

The Motivation List you have generated was also prioritised. This is because almost certainly when it comes down to **What** business do you want to own, you will need to make compromises as not everything on your list will be possible. Trade-offs will be required.

If you know exactly what business you want to own, then you are very lucky. I suspect that most are not 100% sure. For those not 100% sure there are three main facets to consider:

- Passion
- Investment Criteria
- Buy vs Build

Passion

Having something that you are truly passionate about can level mountains, make the impossible seem possible and drive you places you never thought you could achieve. In other words, it gives you an inbuilt motivation to overcome the myriad of obstacles that you will face, if you can combine a passion with a business that is brilliant. What you need to make sure is that the passion can *actually* be turned into a business.

- Is there a market for what you are passionate about?
- Are the economics there for your passion?
- Will it deliver on your prioritised Motivation List?

All important questions. When you run through the Motivation List in detail – how many can be fulfilled by the type or style of business that you are passionate about? Are there other businesses that could fulfil these criteria better?

Passion is a double edged sword – it can drive you to achieve exceptional outcomes but it can also blind you to reality. So you need to make sure that what you are passionate about can really be a viable business. Later in Chapter 7, we look into business plans and this will help you through that process. But at this stage you can look at some simple metrics:

- Are there enough customers who want to buy the services or products you want to supply?
- Are they prepared to pay money for the services/products and the price they will pay will allow you to make a profit?
- Is the cost to acquire these customers going to be less than revenue minus expenses i.e. the profit that you make?

If the above metrics don't stack up, you either need to look harder at your business model or contemplate other options.

Finally, if you did Own a Business that follows your passion, will it actually give you what you are after in terms of your prioritised Motivation List? Let's say for instance, you are passionate about owning a Rhythm & Blues music nightspot but you live in a small town of 10,000 people. You will either need to move to a location with a larger population base or compromise on your passion (or come up with another business model). This may not be a problem if your prioritised Motivation List did not consider location important; indeed you may be prepared to move to New Orleans where there is a ready-made market!

If you are also sitting there scratching your head and not really coming up with anything you are passionate about – don't worry. Having a business aligned to your passion is great, but very few get that real opportunity. There is nothing wrong with having passions outside of your business (although you want to make sure that you are going to enjoy the business because you will be spending a lot of time on it).

A useful process is also looking at the opposite of passion i.e. what do you genuinely hate or dislike. For example, if you are violently against smoking, owning a tobacconist is not the right option for you. What you don't like is sometimes just as important as understanding and knowing what you do like.

Having a passion for something or being passionate against something are useful ways to help filter out what business you want to own.

Investment Criteria

If you don't have a driving passion, how can you select a business to own? In this instance you fall back on the investment criteria (and I should point out this is most common). What you are saying here is effectively, you don't mind what sort of business you run but you are looking at this from an investment point of view. In the previous chapter, when we were looking at the scope we put down a number of what are effectively investment criteria:

- Have a Return on Investment of $[X]
- A target Revenue/ Profit (EBITDA) of $[X] within [x] years
- Needing $[X] to fund the business
- With an exit planned for [x] years or once [y] result has been achieVed
- Owned via the legal entity of [z]

There were other less financially focused criteria but these are still the investment criteria that you are looking at:

- Located at <ideal location>
- In the field of <expertise>
- To help me achieve my goals of [Financial Independence / Save the world / Make Money / Build an Asset for my Family / Create a lifestyle of / Self Determination / Self-Fulfillment]

To achieve your financial and non-financial goals it is often not necessary for you to stick to a particular field of expertise or area. What can be more important is the opportunity, likelihood of success and your confidence.

You need to compare the above with your prioritised Motivation List! To take an example, for me, when I went to look into owning a business, I set down my criteria as follows:

- Nothing more than 4.0 x EBITDA (effectively a ROI of 25%... but this can change depending on finance). Ultimately I wanted to double my investment within 5 years.
- Minimum of $250,000 EBITDA (to keep me living in the lifestyle that I was accustomed to – hah!)
- Needing no more than $1m to fund the business
- Located within 25kms of where I lived – ideally accessible by public transport
- With an exit time frame of 5 years
- Special criteria: Nothing to do with food, not to be dependent on the physical location of the business (i.e. heavy foot traffic required / retail shop front style business unless it was a "sought after destination").
- A business that I could have a clear line of sight as to how I could grow it by at least 5-10% per annum.
- A preference for a business that I had some form of skill, capability or former knowledge in.
- A business that wouldn't rely upon on my sales skills (because I had none)!

You will notice that nowhere did I say what industry I was targeting (I did say what industries I didn't want). I didn't say a cleaning services company let alone a services business. I focused more on the investment criteria and the outcomes that I wanted to achieve. By doing this it opens up the possibilities as to what business I can own.

When you go back to your prioritised Motivation List, unless you have a burning passion for a particular industry, most are not associated with **What** you are going to do. If you are going to have a viable long term business that is profitable, almost certainly you will have staff that will end up doing the day to day physical work. A lot of people never make the leap into owning their own business because they focus far too much on the day to day. Really, you should be focused on the outcomes you are trying to achieve.

Buy vs Build

When I was a project manager, we used to have a saying "Buy the best, build the rest". It is very tempting to run off and start your own business. You have a clean slate, no legacy issues; you can form it to match your specific dreams and goals and it can 100% be yours; a "baby" business that you can nurture and grow. Doing this can be immensely satisfying. But it is also extremely risky. We have previously sprouted out the stats of the incidence of business failure and the percentages of businesses that survive for 5 or more years. When you build from nothing, you are maximising your return but also maximising your risk.

Regardless of whether or not you want to Buy an existing business or build your own, one of the first things you need to do is look at the market. An easy way to do this is to look at businesses for sale.

In Australia there are lots of online sites that can give you streams and streams of businesses for sale. The one I use the most is anybusiness.com.au – this is because it tends to aggregate a lot of the businesses for sale from other sites.

The search functions on most of these sites are pretty poor so don't be upset if you get a large number of results or zero results. The best thing to do is use some criteria and start searching. If you find anything that meets your criteria or is in the same marketplace, then start looking. Do not be frightened to contact the broker.

The process for buying a business is as follows:

- See an advertisement for the sale of the business;
- Contact the owner / broker who has advertised the business;
- Wait for them to respond – at which time they may answer some questions but they should immediately ask you to sign a confidentiality deed;
- You sign the deed;
- They will supply you with an Information Memorandum (IM);
- After viewing the IM you may request to meet with the owners or interrogate the broker further to understand more about the business;
- Many questions may not be answered fully until you actually make an offer;
- Once you make an offer there is normally some haggling around overall terms, etc.;
- Depending on the deal, you may but most likely not, have to put down a deposit;
- Once the "offer" has been accepted, you will undertake (normally, an "exclusive") Due Diligence process. This will depend on the size of the business but starts off at about two weeks but may be as long as 3 months;
- During Due Diligence, the vendor / broker should be able to provide you with as much and as detailed information as you could possibly want;
- At the end of Due Diligence you would either enter into a contract for sale or pull out of the purchase.

To become a business broker you need to hold a licence very similar to a real estate agent's. Having interacted with well over 50 business brokers in my time, I can tell you that the majority share the following characteristics:

- They are very poor at getting back to you. Do not be surprised if they may go days even weeks in responding to your email or phone message;
- They spend a large amount of their day on the phone;
- Just because you get an IM doesn't mean that they will follow up and call;
- Like a real estate agent, they make their money from the seller (in fact they are legally obliged to represent the seller aka Vendor) – so as a buyer they are not there to help you;
- Do not be frightened to call them again and again if you want an answer.

An Information Memorandum is meant to be a document that gives you enough information without giving away trade secrets (like a prospectus or Product Disclosure Statement (PDS) when you are buying a financial product). From this document you should see the following:

- Last 3-5 years of financial results;
- An overview of the market that they operate in;
- (Possibly a) view of impressive companies that they service / sell to;
- An overview of their business, where they operate, how large (staff, turnover etc).

Whether or not you actually wish to buy the business, don't be afraid to ask as many questions as you like. You are under a confidentiality deed so you can't pinch their staff, tell other people about their business (or even that it is for sale) and you can't contact their clients. Despite all of this, you can learn an enormous amount about how a similar business runs and what the challenges are.

The Information Memorandum is meant to be a document of truth so whilst there are large disclaimers over everything, if anything is not truthful in the document, the vendor can be exposed to some liability. Similarly, if during Due Diligence they blatantly lie or give you misleading information, then if you buy the business you may have some legal recourse. The counterpoint to this is that once you end up with lawyers at 20 paces, the only winners are the lawyers.

The key here is, whether or not you are looking to Buy or Build an existing business, this is a great place to start to gather information and a greater understanding about the industry and learn about opportunities out there. You don't even have to limit yourself to a business that meets your direct criteria. It is a great opportunity to get out there and look under the covers of a business. You will be surprised as to what you might learn. It may also open your eyes to other opportunities. My only word of caution is that once you have had a look and if there is no interest, then be clear and direct that you have no further interest – otherwise you might disrupt their sale process which is neither fair nor ethical.

What you will find when you go out there looking is that there are normally lots and lot of businesses for sale. Certainly what I found when I was looking, there was a disproportionate number of franchises for sale. This shows you what a commoditised item they are. If you are at all a student of economics, you will understand the forces of supply and demand. In theory there can be a never ending supply of franchises (they are often limited by geography but that does not stop a similar business opening up next door e.g. McDonalds and Burger King or Hungry Jacks or In and Out Burger, etc). Not only are there existing franchises for sale but also new franchise areas being opened. So tread carefully.

Whether you are looking to Buy or Build, don't be in a massive rush. You are building something that will hopefully be for a long time. If the business you are building or buying, is only going to be successful if you "own" it by a certain timeframe, then you have to worry about the sustainability of the business itself. A seller will always be as keen as possible to close the sale deal as soon as possible but these things take time. A sale can take up to 9 months to a year to execute from start to finish (I have also bought a business in a period of less than 3 weeks from start to finish). What you will find is that opportunities will come and go. So if you miss out on one don't worry, another similar business will be available for sale before you know it. Often, once one industry participant sells, the broker will use that sale to coax other similar businesses into selling.

Another aspect during this investigative process is that you want to cultivate knowledge and information about the brokers. Who is good? Who is responsive? Who is strong in a particular industry? You will also see the different quality of the IMs that you receive. Remember that one day you might be wanting to sell your business and having some inside knowledge as to who the good brokers are, from a buyer's perspective, will certainly help. You may also want to look into some industry consolidation i.e. horizontal integration by buying out some of your competitors, either now or in the future.

Don't forget that when you get to talk to the owners of a business, that you run through your prioritised Motivation List. They would be in the best position to answer what it is like to run their business and how that would meet your list of priorities.

Caution! All business owners have a massive incentive to sell their business. They will almost certainly gloss over the bad bits of running their business. All business owners will underestimate the amount of time that they spend in the business. Phrases such as – "oh I only work part time in the business" or my favourite, "the business basically runs itself, I barely need to be there". This is all BS. After running something for many years, even the worst operator gets more efficient and effective at what they do. Things that take a new owner hours to do, an old hand can do in minutes some times. So whilst they are not necessarily lying they will have glossed over and forgotten how hard it used to be or how hard they used to work. Only a business that has a separate layer of management and a non-owner CEO or General Manager, has a hope of being able to "run itself" – and even then it doesn't "run itself" – a manager runs it!

When considering the buy vs build scenario, you also need to look at any business with a critical eye. Normally when calculating the EBITDA (profit i.e. free cashflow), an existing business will add back a lot of items:

- The D is EBITDA is depreciation – whilst it is valid to add this back, you need to be careful of the flip side which is capital expenditure to be accounted for. When you buy equipment, you need to have the capital available to do so or at least have the finance lined up. As the equipment gets older you depreciate its value. A large depreciation line is normally from a capital intensive business which should demand a lower multiple.
- Addbacks – all owners will add back items – these are anything from personal car use, holidays, parking fines etc. You need to look at these carefully. Some of the favourite ones to add back are:
    - o Advertising expenses – they will normally have some failed advertising campaign or online marketing that "didn't work". Put these back in!
    - o Website development – they will have done a "one off" redevelopment of their website. Once again, a bit of BS. This shows you that you will need to do ongoing development to keep your site fresh and relevant.
    - o Consultants – hmm, what makes you think you won't need consultants in the future?

- o Accountants fees / Booking Keeping fees – they will normally say that you can either do this yourself or they were personal accounts. Add these back in.
- o Owners salary/superannuation +/- family members. With this, you need to be careful as to whether or not you are looking at a business from the perspective of "EBITDA" to the owner or "EBITDA" from a shareholders perspective i.e. are you working in the business or just owning it. Anyone who works in the business will either need to remain or be replaced i.e. either you have to do everything that they do or hire people to replace them. So carefully consider what they do vs what they earn.
- o Just be wary of a business that if it were not for all the addbacks, it wouldn't make a profit. They will claim that this is for tax purposes – but a company that pays tax is a good one – because that means it is earning money!

- Owners "halo". Whether the owner realises it or not, they have a personal impact on a small business. Over the years they will have built relationships, learnt a great deal and become very effective at their job. It is prudent to think that on the revenue line alone, that you will see revenue fall by 10% – (yes, 10%) within the first 12 months, purely from the loss of the existing owner(s). This does not mean that you can't grow the business by this and more over that same time period, but factor this into your thoughts. Even if the owner doesn't realise it, as at the day they sell the business, they are probably one of the most qualified people on the planet to run that business. Doing something for 5+ years at between 50-60 hours a week teaches you a lot whether you realise it or not!
- Expenses – it is rare that an existing business will not have built up some operational fat over time. Expensive mobile phone plans, antiquated equipment that costs more to run than

replace. If you can't find ways to trim some expenses, you are not looking hard enough. On the flip side, any seller who has been planning their exit will have underinvested in equipment, training and put off any discretionary cash outflow possible. So have a bit of spare capital up your sleeve!

A lot of this chapter has been focused on the Buy option rather than the Build. That is because by examining the Buy option, it will teach you more about the Build option than any other form of research. It will also help to validate any business model that you are looking at for a Build – costs, growth, supply side issues, demand side issues, customer needs and wants, personal impacts, seasonal fluctuations etc. You don't know what you don't know; and only by talking to others that have experienced it (or by experiencing it yourself) will help give you that knowledge.

Without a doubt I am biased towards Buying a business rather than building one. The amount it de-risks what you are doing is immense. Even if you don't like a large number of aspects about the potential business you might buy, there is nothing stopping you from being able to change these. The "goodwill" that you are buying i.e. reputation, customer lists, organisational knowhow and knowledge will be worth the expense. This doesn't mean that all business are good to buy and that you can't overpay for a business – not at all – just in terms of risk vs return, it significantly reduces that risk element.

The buy vs build question boils down to the opportunity. By researching and looking into businesses that you can buy, you will have a better understanding of what opportunities exist out there (particularly ones you may not have thought of). You can apply these against your prioritised Motivation List, compare it against what you are passionate about and see how they stack up against your investments criteria. If after all that, you still think you don't have much chance of getting what you want/need, then definitely a build option can be the way to go. Hopefully you will have learnt what makes a successful business in that industry and gathered some intelligence to help structure and form your dream business! Remember Buy the best and Build the rest!

Chapter Summary/Key Takeaways

To work out what business you should seek to own it really comes down to the three things:

- Passion
- Investment Criteria
- The opportunity – Buy vs Build

Even when looking to build your own business from scratch, you can scan and research the existing market and businesses. This will increase your knowledge and improve your chances of success.

At the end of this process you should identify a number of opportunities – when you look at these from the lens of your prioritised Motivation List, hopefully you will have found something (or things) that align. If you don't – then keep looking!

Assuming you have an opportunity in front of you – let's get onto the fun part – Quitting your job!

"Your work is going to fill a large part of your life, and the only way to be truly satisfied is to do what you believe is great work. And the only way to do great work is to love what you do. If you haven't found it yet, keep looking. Don't settle. As with all matters of the heart, you'll know when you find it. And, like any great relationship, it just gets better and better as the years roll on."

—Steve Jobs

Chapter Seven

How to Quit Your Job

"Oh, you hate your job? Why didn't you say so? There's a support group for that. It's called everybody, and they meet at the bar."

—Drew Carey

This seems like a pretty simple question, right? It is easy you just waltz up to your boss raise your middle finger and tell them that you are "out of here". Raid the stationery cupboard on the way out. Done!

Not so fast cowboy. There are lots of simple things that you can do during this part to make the next part of your journey much easier. Now I am making an assumption that you currently have a job – if you don't then I suggest that you still read this chapter (hopefully provide some entertainment). At the very least it should provoke some thought. The main focus for you and quitting your job are the following aspects:

- Timing
- Financial
- Risk reduction

Let's explore these and the ways to manage these to your best advantage.

Timing

You will have set out your schedule as part of the planning process previously. In this you will have put in either a hard deadline or an aspirational goal as to by when you want to be owning your own business. Not everything is always under your direct control and your job is one of those.

One of the first things you should do is find your employment contract. Within this myriad of legalese, there should be something that tells you, your right regarding termination. This should spell out how much notice period you need to give to your employer. If you are a casual employee, you are effectively on a "end of shift" notice period. If I take an Australian point of view then you will most likely have a notice period of 4 weeks; if you are in a senior role or key client facing role then this may be 3 – 6 months. Knowing what this is, gives you a good gauge of what you are up against in regards to time.

The next major step is to determine when YOU want the timing of your employment to end. What are the triggers to making this happen? It is likely that you will have a shopping list of things that you want to make happen before you quit your job:

- Have your finances in place (more on this shortly);
- Have undertaken any training or knowledge mastery you think you need;
- Set up your financial structure;
- Made an offer (and had an acceptance) on the purchase of a business;
- Lifted as much stationery as you can from the stationery cupboard...

In an ideal world when you go to hand in your notice of termination, your boss hands you a cheque for the remainder of your notice period and off you go! This doesn't happen very often but there are still lots of ways that you can engineer this for your own good. The key here is how well you get on with your manager or the person who runs the show.

I would always advocate having an open and honest conversation with your manager to explore the possibilities. This is your chance to see if there are any win wins. When I say open and honest, you don't have to tell them everything you are planning on doing – just that you are looking into leaving your employer to take on some other challenges. It is key during this conversation that you are not actually resigning at that point but giving them some warning that you may be about to do this. A lot of how the conversation goes will depend on the state of the business and how much your manager/ employer values you as an employee. Opportunities that you can explore:

- Are there any redundancies potentially on offer? Whilst it may seem counterintuitive for them to offer a redundancy to someone who is going to leave – good old self interest comes into play. Most parties are given targets of head count reduction and the last thing they want is to make someone else redundant and then lose another person.
- Is there some key work or tasks that they want done before you go?
- Are there some timing opportunities that are important to them if you were to leave i.e. hiring a replacement, get end of year finished etc?
- Could you continue to work part time whilst you start up the business?
- If they need your expertise, are there some options for you to provide some consulting back to them?

Some of the above may depend on what you are looking at doing. Is there a conflict of interest between your current employer and your new business? Are you competitors? Suppliers? Clients? The exact situation will influence what you are able to achieve.

If there is something that they want from you, then you can look to trade this off to your benefit. Even if there isn't an official redundancy, they may be able to create one for you. This would normally be achieved by delaying your departure until a certain date. They may agree if you wait until they find your replacement that at the time of your resignation, they agree to pay out any notice period. Depending on the business they may be able to provide you a guaranteed bonus or some other compensation to delay your plans. Remember that unless you are a casual employee, they can't just sack you because of this conversation. You may reduce future promotional opportunities or pay rises but that is not part of the plan!

The key to remember here is that the timing of your departure is an important bargaining chip that you have with your current employer.

Financial

If you are lucky and you can engineer your departure at the right time and may come along with some bonus cash or maybe a redundancy. There are a few other financial aspects that you need to consider as part of Quitting your job.

- Have you got enough saved up?

  For most people, their job is their primary source of income. Before you toss in the towel and hit the road – make sure that you have enough capital and savings to keep you going for as long as you need. If not, maybe you can work for a bit longer and save a bit more. You have to be realistic; if you are not saving any money while you work then this can be a false safety blanket.

- Annual Holiday / Leave

  Depending on the country you are in, Holiday pay either gets paid out or lost when you leave. If you are in one of those countries where you "use it or lose it" – make sure you take your holidays BEFORE you resign. For those countries that do pay out annual holiday leave, it is a great way to save up extra by not taking any leave and "saving" it up for a final payout. Most countries' employment law is such that, at the point in time you resign, any booked leave is "cancelled" so be aware of this when you come to resign.

- Sick Leave

  I am not aware of any country that pays out sick leave. I don't advocate "chucking a sickie" and using up your sick leave. When you Own your own business, you won't get sick leave – the business doesn't stop when you get sick. So you want to get used to being mentally and physically tough when it comes to being sick.

- Finance

  We will go into some of this a bit more later but simply put – you need to get your finances in order BEFORE you resign. Pay off as many debts as you can, consolidate your savings, pension or superannuation plans. If you need to take out insurance or get a loan, do this whilst you are still an employee. Financial product providers eg banks, are not supportive of people who own their own business. The financial system is geared towards people with a known and regular salary. So do what you need to do financially whilst you still have this regular salary coming in.

- Credit cards/lines of credit

  If you think you might need to have access to some spare cash, occasionally update your credit card limits or obtain lines of credit whilst still an employee. This doesn't mean that you should draw down on these – precisely the opposite – you want to pay off as much of these before resigning.

The key with all of this is that your financial situation will be much easier and simpler when you are an employee. Once you enter the land of the Business Owner, normal rules are suspended and you will be "on your own". So take stock and get as much under control as possible.

Risk Reduction

When you are an employee, your main risks are minimal and well known. It is pretty simple – aside from life threatening situations on the job, your main risk is losing your job. The life of a business owner has a lot more risks. You need to get your mind set as a business owner thinking about the risks or what can go wrong.

To this end, I strongly advocate no matter how much you hate your boss or your job, try and leave on good terms. This is the old adage "don't burn any bridges". You never know when you might have to go crawling back to your old employer and chances are when you do, your finances will be shot to pieces. You need to recognise that owning your own business aside from requiring a lot of work and effort is a risky endeavour.

What other ways can you help to reduce this risk? There are plenty, particularly whilst you still have a job:

- **Training**. Depending on the size of the organisation, chances are there are people and roles that will have or utilise some of the skills that you may need as part of owning a business. Many employees these days have access to online or free training courses. Enrol in as many as you can that are relevant. Offer to work back or do extra work to accommodate the extra time. At the very least, you can find people who work in these roles and talk and "pick their brains" to get a better understanding:

- Sales
- Accounting
- Human Resources/ Industrial Relations
- Customer Service
- Management (people)
- Finance/Budgeting

- **Customers**. Possibly and depending on the type of business that you are going into, your fellow work colleagues could be some of your first customers. Particularly if you are going into a retail business, you can't have too many customers. Remember it is not just them but their family and friends as well. If you are undertaking a B2B operation, your old employer may just be one of your first customers. By seeking these opportunities out whilst you are still employed, you can get a flavour for how hard or easy it will be to sell your products and/or services.
- **Contacts/ Knowledge**. You can often tell when one of your friends has either lost their job or is about to start looking for one – as their LinkedIn profile suddenly jumps with a number of new contacts. Similarly, there is nothing wrong with you enlarging your network, be it on any social media or via other traditional means. You can trawl through who you know and who they know to see if there are connections that can be made. These may be people with vast amounts of knowledge that you can tap. Someone doing you a favour is much more likely to provide you with the real help that you need rather than some pre-programmed consultant looking to extract some service fees.
- **Leaving on good terms**. Your ultimate plan B – return to your job. There are some that believe you should burn your bridges so you can never go back. It may seem like a way to

motivate you, but when you get in there and start running your business you will be motivated enough. So I would advocate to keep the parachute handy and don't throw it out; only to be used when the plane is going to crash, but a small price to pay for a bit of safety. Also you never know when something might derail your plan before you even get out of the blocks – a regulatory change; a purchase of a business falls through, etc., etc. You can't predict the future so keep some options open.

- **Timing**. Only leave when you are ready to start owning your own business. This doesn't mean procrastinating or waiting until all the heavens align. It is more about just planning the time of *when*.
- **Have a break**. You will need all your stamina, energy and mental focus to run your own business. The last few weeks of work are likely to be stressful as you madly hand over knowledge, customers etc. If you are going to start the next day running your business, you will be going out of the frying pan and into the fire. You may not get a holiday for the next 3-5 years, so go ahead and do something fun and enjoyable. Even though they say "a change is as good as a holiday", this will most likely be to an up tempo change and having had a chance to rest and mentally refresh, will be important. The human body is amazing with what it can endure but that doesn't mean you don't want to give yourself the best chance possible.

Emotional Journey

The main points above dealing with the financial, timing and risk reduction are all highly objective considerations. There are of course lots of subjective considerations – the whole act of leaving your job can be an emotionally charged event. An assumption is that only people who hate their job/ boss/

employer are going to want to quit their job and go own a business. In the instance where an opportunity presents itself and you can get the necessary finance in place (see Chapter Eight for more on this), then you have very little to lose in giving owing a business a go. A lot of people will not be in a situation where they hate their jobs and their motivations may not be out of despair or hatred. As we discussed previously, there can be lots and lots of different motivators to wanting to Own a business. It may mean that you are quitting a job that you might enjoy or really like. On top of this you may have a lot of good friends at the workplace that you will potentially miss.

So how best to handle this? It is perfectly normally to feel scared, excited, petrified, nervous and bound by gut wrenching fear. If the leap you are about to make is not having you at least lose sleep for a few nights or having lots of seconds thoughts – then you are probably not stretching yourself very far. I remember when I went to make the big leap, I had a number of sleepless nights worrying myself about whether or not I was making the right decision, what sort of risks was I taking and what sort of an idiot gives up a high paying job that others would dream of one day achieving. Once again, perfectly normal. If it wasn't emotionally hard or financially worrying or not completely risk free – everyone would be doing this. Owning a business is a multi-year commitment, in both time and money. Aside from possibly buying a house, this is likely to be the biggest financial commitment you will ever make (unless you go through this process multiple times).

One key piece of advice is that, don't own a successful small business and operate it part time. Any fanciful notion that you can juggle your existing job and own a business is just asking for trouble. You will most likely end up doing both really badly and at the same time, drive yourself physically and mentally into the ground. You may still choose to mitigate some of your perceived risk by:

- Asking your employer for an extended period of leave without pay, so you can "give it a go" but still have the safety net of a job at the end;
- Asking your employer if you can go part time – just while you start up the business and "prove the concept". This option is only really valid if you are starting a business from nothing. If you are buying an existing business it would be naïve to think that you can do both;
- Asking your employer if you can "contract" back to them occasionally to get some extra cash flow – particularly in the early days.

I am more of a believer in burning the ships! This comes from ancient invaders as they land on foreign shores, burning their ships after landing so that there is no option of retreat, only in going forward. This helps focus the mind only on the future of a successful business.

I have left quite a few organisations in my time. There will always be something or someone that you miss. It is up to you whether or not you continue these relationships. Nothing lasts forever and no matter how much you like something, there are many things out of your control that may take it away from you at any time. Similarly, I have never actually seen someone so important that after they have left the organisation, hasn't coped and found a way to survive without them. Have confidence in what you want to do and make that leap!

Chapter Summary/Key Takeaways

As much as you may not want to, leaving your existing job on good terms is important. Your previous employer may be an important source of customers, ideas and backup plans! With a well thought plan, you can often negotiate an outcome that enables you to trade off timing, financial outcomes and risk mitigation to develop a (hopefully) win-win outcome.

Regardless of the outcome, it is likely that your departure will be an emotionally charged event. It is perfectly natural to feel fear, anxiety and excitement at what you are about to do.

and don't forget to raid the stationery cupboard on the way out...

The next chapter talks about how you can finance owning your own business.

Chapter Eight
How Can I Afford to Own a Business?

"Money is only a tool. It will take you wherever you wish, but it will not replace you as the driver."
—Ayn Rand

Ok, so you now have a plan. You know what you want in a business. You have selected the business you want to own (or at least the key criteria for it). Maybe you even know the exact business you want. You are primed to quit your job. You have made the big decisions! So how do your pay for it? Yikes!

Probably the biggest thing holding most people back in owning their own business, aside from fear of failure, is the ability to fund the start or purchase of a business. This chapter will explore what you can do about that. Working out – how much money i.e. capital, your risk appetite and what you can afford to invest into a business – is critical to your overall decision making process.

If you currently have access to large amounts of capital, that is great. There should be nothing stopping you from going ahead and achieving your dreams and goals of owning your own business. For most people though they probably don't have the capital on tap to do so. So we are going to focus predominantly on those that don't have any capital (or surplus liquid funds) large enough to fund what they want to do. For most, this will mean looking into debt!

Debt is often seen as a dirty word. It is true that there is only one way to go broke and that is not being able to pay back your debts! Despite this, your objective here is to OWN your own business. If you don't have the capital, then debt or borrowing money is the real solution to that. Any debt will have associated regular interest payments and also principal repayments. The alternative to debt is selling off shares – offering people Equity in your business.

When we talk about Equity we are talking about the ownership share you have in the business. The dictionary definition is the "value of shares in a company". We have broadened this as a short form of the relative percentage of ownership in any legal vehicle. This represents the % of a business that you legally own. The ideal is for you to own 100% of a business. Sometimes, to obtain finance you will need to "sell" some of the Equity in a business i.e. the ownership of the business. An Equity owner is entitled to their percentage of any earnings generated by the business and hopefully receive the value of their shares when a business is sold. By selling off Equity in your business, it is already starting to dilute what you are trying to achieve i.e. ownership! This brings us back to the preferred way of obtaining finance – debt.

What you do need to understand is any debt magnifies your risk as well as your return. Many clever financiers will talk about Return on Equity or Return on Investment – technically speaking you don't include the value of debt in these calculations. This isn't necessarily the way you should look at things when owning a small business. Here is a simple example:

- Business Purchase price $100k
- Business Income (Profit) $20k per annum

- Available funds (i.e. Equity/Investment) $20k
- Debt required $80k
- Annual Cost of Servicing Debt $5k

(Ignore all sort of other costs such as transactional costs of purchasing the business etc etc)

The Return on Investment (ROI) is Net Profit / Investment * 100 (as a percentage).

Technically in the example above, your ROI is: (Profit – cost of debt) / Investment amount

($20k -$5k) / $20k *100 = 75%

Now if you were able to invest money and get a 75% annual return, you would do this every single day of the week and you would be borrowing as much money as possible to do so (provided the cost of funding i.e. interest rate was less than 75%). When looking at a small business and the funding, you really need to include the debt as part of the investment – as this is what you are risking. Yes, your business is an asset and conceptually you are buying an asset (and hopefully it will go up in value) – but if it all goes pear shaped, then that asset could be worth $0! A more practical view or a re-worked view of ROI is:

(Profit – cost of debt)/ (Equity + Debt) * 100

($20k -$5k)/ ($20k + $80k) *100 which gives you a ROI of 15% – which is still nothing to be sneezed at.

Always be aware and conscious of the total investment at risk with the purchase or creation of a business. A lender or provider of funds is not going to just forgive what you owe. Hence taking on debt magnifies the return on your capital (i.e. the funds you put in) but also magnifies the risk.

When you start the journey, it is a good idea to start looking into funding early. This will give you an idea of the your ability to source funds which may directly limit or constrain what you can do. Even if you don't know exactly what it is you want to do, understanding what you can afford is very important.

What are the main sources of funds?

- You
- Bank Funding
- Alternative Providers of Funding
- Vendor Finance
- Friends Fools and Family

According to small biz trends the most popular small business financing methods in 2018 were:

- Personal funds: 77 percent;
- Bank loan: 34 percent;
- Borrowing from family/friends: 16 percent;
- Other funding: 11 percent;
- Donations from family/friends: 9 percent;
- Online lender: 4 percent;
- Angel investor: 3 percent;
- Venture capital: 3 percent;
- Crowdfunding: 2 percent.

You will note that it adds up to more than 100% and that is because frequently, people will require more than one source of funds to get the amount of money that they need.

You – and your own personal funds

The option of using your own funds is a bit binary – you either have the funds or you don't. It may sound obvious but if you have the money, you should use it. This will give you the most control over your own destiny and not have you beholden to others. After all, **you** want to Own your own business. Any time you have to use some other source of funds you in some way dilute the level of control you have over either the business or flexibility around running or managing the business. There are a few caveats to this.

The first caveat is you may not have the money. This shouldn't necessarily stop you from using your own funds. It might mean that you need to start building a war chest i.e. savings to allow you to do so. This might form part of your plan as to how you will accumulate these funds. If that seems unlikely or will take too long don't worry – we outline many other options later about how you can get the funds.

The second caveat is even if you do have the money available, you want to keep an eye open to the future. You don't know what opportunities lie ahead or what issues you may face in the future. Even if you do have access to your own capital to "fully" fund the start or purchase of your own business, it is wise to access additional money. There is the old adage, that banks and other financial institutions are only ever willing to lend you money when you don't need it and when you do need it, they won't. This is definitely true and having access to additional funds for that rainy day is a sensible and prudent thing to do!

Bank Funding

"I rob banks because that is where the money is"
—Willie Sutton Outlaw and Bank Robber c.1951 (disputed)

Love them or hate them, banks and major financial institutions (credit unions building societies etc) are a major source of financing. Since the GFC/ Financial Crisis of 07/08 major banks have been less inclined to provide funding towards small business. What you do need to understand is that each bank has its own strategy and its own appetite to take on the risks when lending to small businesses. This appetite can change over time; so in one year, a bank may choose to push further in small business loans and in another year, they may close the doors to new loans. The larger the bank, the more consistent they will be. So often, looking around at some smaller or mid-sized banks may open more doors.

Contrary to popular opinion, banks aren't stupid. They will generally only lend within tight risk parameters that try and create a situation where they minimise the loss of capital. It is important you understand that this is the loss of capital to THEM not to you. They really don't care what happens to you as long as they get their money back!

Depending on the type of business that you are looking at will depend on your options with a Bank:

- Starting a new business. In simple terms you will get nothing out of bank. An idea or a business plan is basically not something that a bank will fund!
- Buying an existing business. A bank may lend to allow a purchase of an existing business. They will need to make a valuation assessment on the business (basically look at the last 3 years profit and take the average) and will generally require a mountain of information:
    - Last 3 years Profit and Loss from an accountant;
    - Last 3 years tax Returns (of the legal entity of the business);
    - Current and proposed balance sheet of the business;
    - Details of your qualifications and or information on previous experience in running a business;
    - Details of your personal assets and liabilities;
    - A Forecast for the business showing Profit and Loss for the next 2 years.

- Franchises. This is where buying an existing or setting up a new franchise has its benefits. Quite frequently a franchisor will have already made arrangements with one or more financial institutions as to how you can borrow money to purchase one of their franchises. This is done on the basis that the franchise model should increase your chances of being able to run a successful business. As part of the process of becoming a franchisee the franchisor will effectively undertake the same level of checks as a bank might do re you having the finances and also the skills to run one of their businesses. As part of this process they will also provide training and support as to how to run the business effectively. Banks recognise this and "reward" this by having preferential predetermined treatment around the business. It also means that they have a third party (albeit biased) that can validate future cashflow and earnings forecasts.

The above gives you a generalised view of how a bank will treat lending to a business but it is not the way they actually view it.

Ultimately a bank looks at the security provided against the loan and the ability to repay a loan. In bank speak they divide loans in to Unsecured and Secured loans. A Secured loan is a loan that is specifically tied to a piece of real property ie an asset. This could be a Residential property (a commercial property), a piece of equipment, motor vehicle etc etc. In Australia a Residential property sits on top of the pile in terms of assets with borrowing value. Anything that has a unique identifier (eg a serial number, vehicle chassis, registration number etc) can be lodged in the Personal Property Security Register (PPSR) and be provided as security for a loan. Just because it can be registered doesn't mean that a bank will accept it as a viable form of security though. A bank will be prepared (in general) to lend you more money against a secured loan. Why is this? Well it is pretty straight forward – the act of securing the loan against an asset (via the PPSR or Registering a mortgage against a property) this prevents the owner (in theory you) from selling or disposing of the asset without the Bank's permission ie paying off the loan. It also means that in the instance that you default on the loan or go bankrupt – no one else can sell that asset without first paying off the loan (and any default fees, interest, legal fees – for the bank etc etc). So the Bank is the first in the queue (for that asset) to recover whatever funds that they need. This is why they value having security – it reduces the risk that they don't get their money back.

The other type of loan is an unsecured loan. Like the name says you are not putting up any form of security. The bank will look a lot harder at the risk of providing the loan. This means looking at what assets may exist in the winding up of a company and also your personal assets. Whilst on the surface it sounds as though they are lending without any form of security – it is not really the case. An unsecured loan means that in the event of you defaulting or going bankrupt they join the queue along with everyone else to recover their money. This means that is it less likely that they will get all of their money back. Banks have an even better way of making sure that they get their money back – the Directors guarantee.

Let me explain. Most small businesses are likely to be set up as a limited liability corporation or in Australian speak a Proprietary Limited company (normally abbreviated to Pty Ltd). This means that any liability is limited to the assets within the company. One or more Directors is responsible for running the company. As long as the directors don't commit fraud and don't trade whilst insolvent, the buck stops at the company. So in a simple example, if the Company borrows $100k, paying 10% per annum and at some point it becomes apparent that they are not making enough money to be able to pay back the loan or the interest bill i.e. "cannot pay its debts as and when they are due", the Directors may be forced to wind up the company or bring in administrators. If there is insufficient value or assets in the company to pay back the loan, then the liability for that loan stops at the company i.e. the lender is out of pocket not the owners etc. There are other examples of this that don't apply to loans – you might get an adverse court ruling which means that the company has to pay millions in damages – either uninsured or can't pay. In this instance, if the company can't pay, the Directors would once again wind up the company. The liability of that payment would stop at the company. The owners i.e. shareholders would be free of these "debts".

With the above examples (and others), this is where the Directors guarantee comes in. Banks and other financial institutions, being the clever people that they are, have worked out a way to avoid the problems highlighted above when businesses fail. When you take out a business loan, Unsecured or Secured, they will almost certainly have you sign a Director's guarantee. This is a personal guarantee that you will pay the bank back the money you have borrowed. So for the debts owed to the bank, they can reach beyond the company and seek to reclaim funds by forcing (via the courts) for you to sell or hand over other assets that you own, that are not linked to the company.

(Before you get too freaked out by this, it is worthwhile mentioning that in Australia, when you take out a normal Mortgage to buy a residential property, the loan you take out is a full recourse loan. This means that in the event of a default on your mortgage, not only can the bank sell your home to recover funds, it can also come after any of your personal assets as well. In other countries such as the USA, most home loans are on a non-recourse basis i.e. the banks can only take possession of the security provided for the loan and they can't seek "recourse" against the borrower.)

The important point about this, is understanding the risks that you take on by borrowing money from a bank (and most other financial institutions are more likely to be worse). Even though you may think by its name that a loan is unsecured, you will still be putting at risk, your assets! Simply put, they will not let you take out an unsecured loan without providing a Directors guarantee, or a personal guarantee if you are not a director. Similarly, you might think that you are only offering up a specific set of assets when you have a Secured loan but the almighty Directors guarantee means that in the event of a wind up, the bank can come after ALL your assets and even put you into personal bankruptcy! (They can only recover funds to the amount that they are owed – they can't take more than this. BUT any expenses that they incur in recovering the funds can also be recovered i.e. their legal fees, default fees, normal interest and default interest etc – once you get in default, the amount owed multiplies very, very quickly.)

As you can see, debt is a double edged sword – it increases your opportunities to own a business but also increases your overall risks!

The actual amount that a bank will lend will vary from year to year, and bank to bank. But here are the basic parameters that you can look at:

	Unsecured	**Secured**
Loan to valuation ratio	Maximum 50% of the value of the business	Maximum 80% of the value of the Security i.e. the asset, normally a property
Maximum amount	No real maximum but generally the sweet spot is between $250k and $1m	No real maximum – depends on security
Can borrow for a new business?	No… or it is really, really hard	Yes
Can borrow for a new franchise	Yes	Yes
Term	Maximum of 7 years. Normally linked to the tenure of the lease of the business premises	Can be as long as a residential mortgage, but normally 15 years.
Interest Rate less than $200k	12-15% per annum	8%+
Interest Rate	6-8% Generally, 3-4% greater than standard mortgage rate	5-6% Generally, 1-1.5% greater than standard mortgage rate
Interest Only	No. Amortised i.e. reducing balance over term of loan	Not normally. But may be able to get up to a 3 year interest only period.
Income Requirements	Ability to have business make repayments + able to cover personal income needs and expenses of a business. Repayments would be 20% of income	Ability to have business make repayments + able to cover personal income needs and expenses of a business. Repayments would be 20% of income

	Unsecured	Secured
Settlement Fee	Normally about 1% of amount loaned	Normally about 0.5% of the amount loaned + Security registration fee
Director's Guarantee	Yes. Mandatory	Yes. May be able to avoid if amount loaned is less than, say, 50% of security
Documentation required	Business Valuation Last 2-3 years trading history 2 year future forecast Business Plan Proof of owners qualifications/ industry experience in business Overarching Business Case as to why bank should lend funds	Security Valuation Proof of ownership of security Proof of income Business plan
Time frames	1-2 weeks to prepare submission 2 weeks Bank review – obtain conditional approval 2 weeks Due Diligence 2 weeks settlement	2-3 business days – obtain conditional approval 2 weeks due diligence 2 weeks settlement

How does a bank value an existing business? It is not that complicated. They will in general, look at the following things:

- Why are the existing owners selling? This is to capture any red flags i.e. the business has undisclosed problems or is the business in trouble. Any signs of problems and the banks will decline.

- Last 2 years earnings (backed by Tax Returns and in Australia, Business Activity Statements or BAS). They take the average of the earnings for the last 2 years. Sometimes they require last 3 years earnings. Stability in earnings is more valuable than a high growth rate!
- Growth potential + contracts that "guarantee" turnover and earnings.
- Size of business. Larger businesses are seen as more valuable as they can weather economic fluctuations better.
- Apply some multiple on the above factors.

Frequently a bank will rely upon an independent business valuation (that way they can sue someone else or blame someone else if something goes wrong). Most business brokers are also licensed to provide business valuations as well.

The other good thing about banks is that once you understand their "rules", as long as you work within them you can twist these to your own advantage. A great example is that you can "double dip" with a bank loan. If you have a secured loan, they will lend you up to 80% of its value. Great. You can then take out an unsecured loan as well – to the value of 50% of the business. Through this mechanism you could conceptually borrow even more than 100% of the purchase price of a business! You would still need to prove that you have sufficient income to service the debt. This can even be taken further with credit cards, personal loans etc. I am not encouraging you to take out unnecessary debt, just pointing out that with a bank, once you are in the door and seen as an acceptable risk – they want you to borrow as much and more expensive debt as possible (as long as you can afford it)!

Here's a final note on bank lending. Security is the key with obtaining good bank financing. For most people, this will be residential property – normally their home. You need to enter into doing this with the understanding that you are placing your home at risk – but without risk there isn't reward!

Alternative Providers of Finance

Banks are not the only providers of finance. The best way to manage alternative providers of finance is to go through a broker. A finance broker that specialises in funding for businesses is almost a necessity to understand and weave your way through the complexities, rules and bureaucracy that you are likely to face. Also note that a finance broker will also help to get you access to bank finance as well.

Finance brokers don't do this out of love. They will charge a fee that normally they can get rolled into the loan, for their services. This will generally be $750 -$1500, depending on the size of the funds required and then a success fee that is a percentage of the funds acquired – normally 0.5%-1% for unsecured funding and 0.5% for secured funding. This difference in the amounts will generally reflect the amount of paperwork required. They will shoulder the lions' share of documentation preparation and they will have all the knowledge about how best to prepare all the financiers forms!

What are the other types of finance?

- Equipment/ Vehicle and Fit Out finance
- Factoring
- Non-Bank Lenders
- Home Loan

Equipment and fit out financing is normally provided by a leasing arrangement. Leases generally come in two types Operating and Finance leases. The main difference between the two is that with a finance lease, at the end of the lease you are the owner of the equipment; with an operating lease, at the end of the lease you return the goods to the lessor. Leases work well when you have a well-defined asset (not normally a property). You have two parties to a lease – a Lessor (the person providing the funds) and the Lessee (the person borrowing the funds). A Lessor effectively has security (or even ownership of the asset in the case of an Operating lease) over the asset in question. Similar to the other secured forms of lending, this gives them the right to the asset in the case of a default. Where a lease is also beneficial is that in most countries, they have some taxation benefits but the real power is that the lessor should align the lease so that the amount outstanding on the "loan" is the equivalent to the value of the asset at the end of the term. This fancy process of reducing the balance of a loan is called Amortisation! Let me give you an example:

Say you want to buy a car that costs $40,000, just for argument sake, let's say the interest rate was 6% per annum (0.5% per month). Most lenders on a car would only give you a maximum 5 year loan. Let's assume that there is an expectation that the car would be worth $20,000 at the end of 5 years. Based on a fully amortised loan (i.e. the amount owing after 5 years is $0), over a 5 year period you would be making payments of approximately $773 per month. With a lease, you would only need to pay $487 per month. So a lease reduces the amount of cashflow you have to provide each month to utilise the asset. With operating leases etc, you also have the benefit that you can "return" the goods at the end of the lease and get brand new models at the end of the time period.

If that doesn't make entire sense don't get too worried at this stage. What you need to understand is that for any business, you are likely to require a number of assets that you will be using:

- Cars, trucks – any sort of vehicle
- Computer Equipment
- Site fit out/ furniture
- Equipment and tools

For any assets that are worth at least $300 and over, you can probably find a bank or financier that will be prepared to lease these to you. They can probably also provide a chattel mortgage or some other form of security loan if required as well. More often than not with leases, you can get 100% of the amount of the equipment financed – you don't need a deposit. If you are finding that the more traditional forms of finance are not readily accessible, leasing is often an easier path of financing – especially if your business is equipment intensive. You will still need to provide some level of documentation but normally the documentation requirements are a lot less. A basic forecast or historical set of numbers for the business will be sufficient. Depending on the maturity of the business and the overall balance sheet, you can get away with not having to provide a Directors guarantee on a lease or equipment finance. If you don't have any trading history, this will be a lot harder.

You can also do this for any fit out. For example, if the business that you are looking at – say, for a restaurant or any retail shop front style operation – you are likely to need invest in a fit out for the premises. This is very helpful for starting a business as the fit out costs are likely to be one of the largest expenses you will have. If you are purchasing an existing business, you can also get the existing fit out valued and borrow against it. You might be surprised at what sort of value you can get out of assets from within the business as security for some form of finance. Similar to leases, the lender is used to this type of arrangement and the ease of obtaining funds is generally easier. A note however, is that there is a materiality to any of these forms of obtaining finance – if the amounts (in total) are small, then the lender is not likely to be interested in the piece of business.

Factoring. This form of financing, particularly at the start of a business, is generally harder to obtain. The act of Factoring (or occasionally called Debtor Finance) involves the lender buying your accounts receivables i.e. your invoices or contracts with clients at a discount and providing you with the money up front. For example, if you have invoiced a "credit worthy" client or have a contract with pre-defined payments, you can sell these commitments from your clients. In general, depending on the credit worthiness of the client, a Factoring party can buy these future cashflows at about a 6% discount to their face value. They will also provide the "service" of collecting this money from the clients. When you think about it ,you are selling your invoices to get the money upfront – saving yourself maybe 2-3 months of waiting to get the cash for a 6% fee. Those keen beans will have worked out that you are basically borrowing money at a rate of between 24 and 36% per annum! But if you are short of cash and need funding, particularly if you have strong clientele and large dollar value invoices, it can be a viable way of obtaining funds in advance. This is much more viable if you are buying an existing business; they have pre-existing client commitments or contracts and the dollar value of invoices are high.

Non-Bank Lenders. Not really that much different to the bank lenders. The main difference is that they are more likely to specialise specifically in lending to businesses. Unless you have personal connections in this space, this is almost certainly done through a broker. Non-bank lenders are likely to have different risk criteria and since they will more likely specialise in the type of finance, they will be able to handle more unusual cases. Their cost of funds, for their business, is likely to be higher than what the banks are likely to be paying, so don't be surprised if they charge higher interest rates. Like a bank, they are not a charity organisation. Where they do have an upside, is the tolerance for risk e.g. they will often provide a Secured loan with a valuation ratio of up to 90% of the asset. During boom times this can get as high as 100%!

There are also a growing number of online lenders who offer business loans. These are not generally relevant to either starting up a business from scratch or purchasing an existing business. They normally rely upon detailed analysis of how the business is currently running. Until you have a trading history, it will be difficult to meet their requirements.

Home Loan. Technically you will still be approaching a bank or your current lender. Not applicable to everyone but if you have your own home and have built up some equity in your home loan, then refinancing your existing home loan can be one of the easiest and cheapest ways to get funding. The key to this, is being smart about how you undertake the application:

1. Obtain a valuation of your current property. Even if you ask a real estate agent about how much they think your property could sell for, this will give you a fairly good idea. A bank will always seek an independent assessment as well.
2. Determine the current loan to valuation ratio of your existing mortgage and the current value of your home. You calculate this as follows:

   Current Mortgage/ Value of Home x 100%

3. In simple terms, if your current mortgage is less than the value of the home then the gap between the two is how much you can borrow using your property as security. Ideally you only want to borrow as much as what would take your loan to valuation ratio (calculated in 2 above) up to 80%; but many lenders might allow you to borrow up to 105%!
4. Assuming that you have some room in terms of borrowing power, you want to approach your existing lender about how you might be able to borrow more. If the existing lender isn't agreeable then approach other lenders.
5. The key is that you need to do this BEFORE you quit your job i.e. whilst you still have a normal salary. Banks and lending institutions treat earnings of an employee as being

far more stable and reliable than earnings from a business. When you take out a loan, just like a Secured business loan, they look at two key things – the security provided i.e. the value of your home and your ability to repay the loan. When you still have a job, your *current* pay is how they work out ability to repay the loan.

6. If you are required to explain WHY you wish to refinance and borrow more funds, the suggestion would be to "invest in shares" – this is not technically incorrect. It is just that they will most likely assume that you are talking about listed shares. They may inquire about which listed shares and the main reason for this would be to include their dividend stream as part of your income. They may also try and get you to take out a margin loan instead – do not do this. It is a risky way to obtain finance and combine that with potential risks of owning a business, it is a recipe for disaster.
7. It is recommended that you find out the maximum amount you could borrow via this mechanism. At this point in time it is always best to obtain as much capacity to borrow as you can. You can always pay it back or make additional repayments early.
8. Most lenders will allow you to create "sub" loans – probably with their own loan identification number. If you do proceed to refinance and take out a loan, you should structure the borrowing so that the existing amount of the mortgage is held under one account and the new funds that you intend to use for starting or buying a business are held under another account. The reason for this is that most countries allow the interest expense of loans that are for income producing purposes, to be tax deductable. To enable this to apply, you have to keep the funds segregated and be able to show that the purpose of the loan is not for the purpose of personal use i.e. it has an income producing intent.

9. Take out the loan and set up a re-draw facility or an offset account. Any funds that you don't need immediately for the business should be either paid back (to reduce your interest expense) or placed in the offset account.

You should always seek accounting and tax advice on this so that it is setup as practically as possible. The use of your home as security does place your home at risk in the event of a business failure but it also provides you with one of the most cost effective and painless ways to obtain access to significant levels of funding (interest rates on home loans are always a lot cheaper than commercial business loans). Remember that with other forms of finance, you will most likely be forced to provide a Directors guarantee anyway, so whether you realise it or not, your home is still at risk!

Vendor Finance

If you able to access it, Vendor Finance is one of the simplest means to obtaining finance for the purchase of an existing business. What is Vendor finance? Simply put, it is the existing owner of a business, agreeing to lend you money to purchase their business. Whilst this may seem counterintuitive, it happens frequently. Why would a vendor do this? There are many reasons:

- By providing vendor finance they can speed up the sale process;
- Increase the number of potential purchasers;
- Maximise the purchase price of the business;
- A strong show of faith in the ongoing fortunes of a business.

Normally a vendor would only provide vendor finance up to 50% of the purchase price of a business, but there are no rules like what you would see in a bank. A lot will depend on the reasons for a sale. For example, if someone wants to retire or they are sick or injured, by offering up Vendor Finance, it can rapidly increase the number of parties that can afford to buy the business. They may like the idea of still being able to "profit" from the ongoing operations of the business.

Vendor Finance is normally short-ish term in nature, it being a term of 2-3 years. It is generally interest only payments but with some possible balloon payments along the way. The interest rate charged is generally 2-3% above what you pay for an equivalent duration Term Deposit. Once again, you are not dealing with a bank that has rules but an existing owner who is looking to make a return. The interest rate and term will largely depend on the Vendor; they can set what they want. It will almost always "cost" more than an equivalent level of bank financing.

If you are a buying a business, it is always a good question to ask if they would be prepared to provide Vendor Finance. Regardless of whether or not you are interested in taking up the offer, it is informative to listen to their response. If the seller is not prepared to offer it up it may be a red flag about the business; it asks the question "if they are so confident in the future prospects in the business, why wouldn't they?" There are lots of valid reasons – they wish to use the money for other purposes, they don't trust the ability of a new owner to run the business (which is a side worry) or they have debts to pay off. Either way you learn something. It may also provide some options.

There are some variations to Vendor Finance that are not "finance" per se. They are:

- **Deferred settlement**. This is where you agree to pay a portion of the price of the business up front and then have a staggered payment plan. This allows you to use the cash flow of the business to ideally build up additional capital. It also allows you to have some trading history develop to enable you to apply for other forms of normal borrowing from banks etc. You need to be careful that either you have a sufficiently lengthy time frame to accumulate the capital or have a reasonable confidence in your ability to raise the funds. You don't want to be in the position to miss a settlement payment. There are often hefty penalty interest clauses for late payment and conceptually with a bit of legal action, the seller can take back the business! Despite the risks, this is a great way of gauging the confidence of the seller in the business and also minimising the amount of capital required. Be careful though, with most banks as part of the settlement, will want to see the purchase contract and will be wary if you have a deferred settlement amount, as this could lead to defaults – or more importantly from their point of view, trouble repaying their loans!

- **Earn Outs.** An Earn Out is where the payment amount of the business is tied to the future earnings of the operations. As a buyer of a business, this is a fantastic way to buy a business. It also normally involves the remaining exiting owners, to work in the business for some time. It is normally only used when the purchase of the business is in the multiples of millions – it is quite rare for smaller businesses. Once again why would a seller do this? It may be the only way that they can get a buyer but also the best way to maximise the sale price. If a seller has huge confidence in the future earnings and opportunities, or even the team that they have put in place to run the business, they may opt for an earn out. This also allows them to share in the upside of the business as it goes forward. The earn out portion is generally only 10-20% of the final purchase price, so the buyer still has to have the majority of the funds available. Most sellers would much prefer to provide a deferred settlement or some form of Vendor Finance rather than go for an Earn Out. The key problem (benefit if you are the buyer) is that as the seller, you have lost control of the business but are still on the hook to deliver the results.

As listed above, Vendor Finance is of great benefit to the buyer but on the surface has lots of risk to the seller and reduces the immediate access to a portion of the purchase price. So how do you encourage them to provide Vendor Finance? If you look at it from a sellers point of view, they would much prefer:

1. No Vendor Finance, over
2. Vendor Finance, over
3. Deferred Settlement, over
4. Earn Out.

Using the above, you can always make multiple offers for the business that have a variety of the above combinations. You need to be careful that all are acceptable to you. Here is an example for a business where the owner is seeking a purchase price of $500k, turnover of $1m per annum.

1. An offer of $450k upfront payment + other terms
2. An offer of $250k upfront and $225k of vendor finance paying 6.5% interest per annum with a term of 3 years (probably amortising) + other terms
3. An offer of $500k with $200k paid upfront and $50k paid every 6 months for the next 3 years.
4. An offer of $300k upfront with 10% of turnover paid each 12 months for the next 2 years.

All of the above offers are +/- mathematically equivalent. They all result in the seller getting about $500k in total after 3 years. A seller can reject them all but by presenting a number of options, you can flesh out what is important to them and use that to either reduce the sales price or get the finance that you may need.

Overall the tips to getting them to the point of providing Vendor Finance are:

1. Look to maximise their sales price. If you are prepared to pay more than other interested parties, then they will be more inclined to give you vendor finance.
2. Use it to speed up the process. Most sellers will supposedly have a genuine reason as to why they wish to move on – so offering them a quick exit should be of real interest to them.
3. Stand firm and only provide an offer requiring some form of finance from them. This has the potential to remove you as an interested purchaser.

With Vendor Finance you will almost certainly need to provide some level of up front funding. It does however, give you a real chance to be able to purchase a business that would not be in your price range by having the Vendor provide you with the funds. Vendors are less likely to require Directors guarantees, but they will almost certainly secure it against the business i.e. in the event of default, they will take the business back. Not all sellers will offer it up but combined with a quick sale and high offer price, they will often agree to the terms.

Friends, Fools and Family

I can safely say that at various times in my life I have been a Friend, a Fool and a Family member in providing funds to people wanting to own their own businesses. Does that make me stupid? Maybe. The good news for you is that I am not alone in doing this.

No matter what demographic you come from, you are bound to know someone who has access to money. Whatever happens, no matter how wealthy they are, you need to respect that this is their money (hard earned or otherwise) and they have the upper hand as they have something that you need!

Why would they contemplate doing this?

- They may like you and have a vested interest in wanting you to do well;

- They may trust you;
- Like you, they may be passionate or have a deep-seated interest in what your business is going to do;
- Financial return.

Whilst many people may disagree with me, what you really want to do is borrow money from them to either purchase the business you want to own or help finance the start of the business. You are not creating some multi-million dollar highly scaleable Start-up (or at least that is not what this book is really about). For high risk "shoot for the moon" Start-ups, selling Equity i.e. shares in the business, is a viable strategy as the extremely high levels of risks can be offset by the potential (low probability) enormous returns.

Presumably one of the key reasons that you like the idea of owning your own business, is that you have control and also ownership of an asset. If you start selling off equity then you are diluting your control and most importantly diluting your level of ownership. Where ever possible, unless they are actively going to work with you in (or on) the business, you don't want equity partners. The other exception would be if the amounts of dollars that you are asking for are substantial and the amount of money that you can bring to the table is minimal or non-existent (then you may be forced to offer up some portion of equity). Ideally if you do this, you need to have a clear documented (and signed) agreement outlining the terms. Within this, you want to have clear terms whereby you can buy this equity back if required.

The above is *why* you should be looking at borrowing money i.e. getting a loan from them. To get a loan, you are not likely to have to go through as many hoops as a bank or financial. Ultimately it will come down to how much they trust you as to whether or not they will provide funds for you. A smart Friend, Fool or Family (FForF) will probably require the same set of security or guarantees that a bank would (and you should not be offended if they ask for these). If you aren't prepared to give them these then that shows a lack of faith in what you are doing!

Any interest rate or terms is likely to come down to what they need, to compensate them for the risk that you may represent. For a business loan, you can expect that they will be looking for a 2-3% premium over what you may get from a bank. It will also depend on the opportunity cost for them i.e. what sort of return are they getting from their funds elsewhere. It is unrealistic for you to expect that they will pull their money out of an existing investment to earn *less* than what they currently do! The other thing to note here is that you have a real opportunity to get flexible terms. An example might be that if you are starting up a restaurant and funds are required for fitting out the premises, you may have no income to pay interest / principal on the debt for the first 6 months. In this instance, you can agree that no repayments are made for the first 6 months. Similarly, if your business is seasonal, you can structure the interest payments to reflect that seasonality.

So how do you go about doing this? Here are the steps that I suggest:

- Make a list of all the wealthy people that you know. Make a note of how much you think that they are worth and how much disposable funds they can access. Also note if they are a Friend, Family or Fool. Think about why they might be prepared to help.
- Make sure that you have your business plan in place that shows what you hope the business will be able to achieve in terms of revenue and profit and over what time frame.
- In the context of your plan and forecasts, come up with a term sheet for the debt, in other words :

  - o How much do you need?
  - o What sort of interest rate are you prepared to pay?
  - o Term i.e. duration
  - o How will interest payments and repayments work?
  - o Show that you can afford to make the payments in accordance with your term sheet and make sure you work these back into your business plan.

- Come up with a **pitch** as to what you need and why.
- Start talking to your friends first as they are more likely to give you constructive feedback.
- Take any feedback and work it back into the plan, term sheet and the pitch.
- Once you have a comfortable and sensible proposition, start working through the list of Friends, Family then Fools. You want to start with those that you think a) are more motivated to lend you the funds; b) have access to the amount of funds that you require. Ideally, you would rather have one lender than many. Having too many parties that you have to pay back makes ongoing management of your debt much more difficult.

For any such debt taken out, you will want to have a clear, well documented (signed) loan agreement put in place. I recommend using an online platform like *credi.com*. This allows you to create the contract and also, calculate and track the ongoing interest and repayments in a clear way to both parties. This can also put in place appropriate mechanisms for when things go wrong!

There is no doubt that borrowing money from people that you know is not only risky for them but also places at risk whatever relationship that you have with them. Nothing tests a relationship better than having arguments over money!

The FForF path can often be a path of last resort. You are likely to find that you will be paying a higher price, in terms of interest, but you can often offset this with flexibility on terms. They will generally do this because they trust that you will be able to repay them (so you need to make sure that you do!).

Can you use FForF in conjunction with other finance? Simple answer is yes. The financial institutions may have a requirement to understand if you are using any other borrowings. The main reason they will be interested in this, is to make sure that they get "first bite of the cherry" in the case of a default. This will be less of an issue to them if security (for their loan) is in place.

Chapter Summary/Key Takeaways

The main message to take away from this chapter, is that there are a blistering array of ways to obtain finance to own a business. Important questions to ask are, how much you are comfortable in borrowing and how much do you think you can get? These questions should be answered as you go about deciding what sort (and size) of business you want to own. You will be amazed at what you might be able to get finance for. Sources of finances can nearly always be found – it just depends on your ability to find them and what price (interest) you will need to pay to get it:

- Banks and Financial Institutions: Via secured and/or unsecured loans. Normally, the lowest interest rates but the hardest and more time consuming to get;
- Alternative Finance: Equipment Financing/ Invoice Factoring. Hard to get large amounts but can help to provide the finance that you need;
- Vendor Finance: A great way to get access to some of the funds that you need often on favourable terms. Not always an option;
- Friends, Fools and Family: Deep pockets from people that you know. Can be flexible but is normally expensive. Comes down to how much they trust you!

The next chapter is going to look in to the all-important Business Plan!

Chapter Nine

Have You Got a Business Plan?

"A goal without a plan is just a wish."
—Antoine de Saint-Exupéry

"If you don't know where you are going, you'll end up someplace else."
—Yogi Berra

No matter what you do with owning your own business, at some point you are going to need a business plan. This does not have to be "War and Peace" and it can be as simple as a spreadsheet but a business plan you will need! If you are going for financing from another party, one of the first things that they ask for is your business plan.

A business plan in simple terms outlines the following:

- An overview of the business and your business model- what products and services you are offering and how will you make money;
- Target market – who is going to buy from you;
- Value Proposition and your competition;
- Sales and Marketing;
- Business structure – legal framework, ownership;
- Operating plan – organisational structure, resource, equipment;

- Financial summary – including financing requirements;
- Supporting research and information.

As much as the plan itself is important, the act of sitting down and working out the above information is actually far more valuable to you as a business owner. This will help to give you an understanding of what the business is trying do and how it is going to achieve it.

The good news is that there are hundreds of templates out there that you can download for free. Government departments, banks etc have lots of good examples that you can use. Most will be very similar. The look and presentation of the business plan is not important. Don't waste your time making it look pretty. Anyone who is going to seriously look at your business plan doesn't care what it looks like – they are going to be ten times more interested in its contents.

Grab yourself a template of a business plan and let's get started at populating the contents.

Business Overview

This isn't an executive summary but a short series of statements about what the business is. If you are buying an existing business this is easy. In their Information Memorandum (IM), they should have provided you with a whole section on what the business is and how it works. Don't be shy in lifting as much information as you can out of their IM. The plagiarism police won't be marking you on this one. Indeed (aside from imitation being the most-sincere form of flattery) – ultimately you will be better off using a business model that has been proven to work.

An area where an IM often glosses over, is on the how it works. This is a simple understanding about how the money machine in the business functions. It may be simple but if you don't understand this, you will struggle to make a successful business.

This means knowing – what are the inputs, where do you get them from, what do you do with them and what are the outputs.

Let's take an example of a chicken shop – Plucky Plucker (PP) chicken shop:

Target Market

Understanding your market is very important for your business. This is who and where you are going to sell to. The key with your business overview is keeping it short and clear but also presenting the reader with a clear understanding of what it is that the business does and how it intends to make its money. The above example took a relatively simple retail style product. If you were to take something a bit less structured, say an Engineering Consulting business, you can still break it down as well. With a service or consulting style business, your inputs are your staff and any equipment or consumables they need to do their job. The outputs are the service and subsequent payments made by the customers. Frequently, businesses will have elements of manufacturing (eg cooking the chicken), products/retailing (eg pre-packaged drinks) and services (eg dine in).

There are many ways to describe or identify your target market. Why is it important to understand this? Well if you don't know enough about your target market, you won't know what their needs are and how to connect with them. The more you know and understand your target market, the better positioned you are to tailor your product offering and any marketing and advertising activity. There is a temptation to see your target market as everyone or every business but the reality is that you are operating a small business (unless you have an unlimited advertising budget, you need to get smarter about who you target). The better defined and the better understanding you have of your target market, the easier it will be for you to generate business.

How is a target market normally defined? Quite often people describe a "persona" of a typical person or type of person that will buy your products and services. This also makes the target market experience more relatable. Let's take an example for the chicken shop PP:

Persona: Maggie the Mum

Description: Maggie is between 35 and 45; she is a busy working mum that is time-poor and has at least one, but often 2 kids in tow. She lives locally and has enough disposable income to allow her to "eat out" once or twice a week. She likes the idea of having her kids eat "healthy food" so likes to try to avoid too much fast food. Cares about her community and the environment.

It may be that your business has a few different personas that it targets, possibly corresponding to different times of the day or different products and services that you have. The more specific you can be, the better chance you have of finding your target market and understanding their needs better.

Other ways to describe your target market are more demographically focused:

- Age
- Gender
- Income
- Location
- Behaviour and Lifestyle
- Values
- Interests

If you are buying an existing business, the existing owners, either in their IM or through discussion, should be able to articulate who their target market is. Otherwise you can look at what your competitors are targeting to see what they have defined their target market as. Other ways to understand this better are looking into what problems or needs your products and services solve. You can look at existing customers and see if there are patterns or trends in the type of customers that buy from the business. You can even ask your customers! Understanding why people buy from your business is a very important piece of information. This understanding may also drive greater insights and open new opportunities!

Once you have determined your target markets, it is important that you validate your product/services against this. You may have identified the perfect target market but is it large enough and can it afford your products/services? Often you will be part of an overall market – so understanding the total market size is still a useful point. This can also give you an idea of the growth in the overall category. You will then need to try and understand, if possible, where your target market fits within this. The size and cost to attract your target market has been the downfall of many businesses. If the target market is insufficient to sustain your business, you will be doomed from the start. If we take our erstwhile chicken shop as an example – if Maggie the Mum is time-poor, she is unlikely to want to travel more than 2-3 kms (or more accurately has to spend more than 5 minutes in a car!) hence anything more than this and she is unlikely to make the effort. If within that zone, there are only 500 dwellings and local demographics are that 50% of residents are single person families, then the chances are there will be insufficient Maggies to sustain your business. There are of course ways around this – home delivery service etc (I think you get the point).

Value Proposition and Competition

With your knowledge of your target market, you can now try and articulate your value proposition! Your business' value proposition is (hopefully) a clear statement about what it is you offer that makes customers want to buy from you. It goes by other names such as USP – Unique Selling Proposition, Product differentiation, etc. Whilst it would be nice to have a catchy phrase, a little bit akin to your mission statement – for a small business, a simple list of the qualities of your products and services, is more practical.

Before you launch too far into defining the business' Value Proposition, it is a worthwhile exercise understanding where your competition sits. No matter what business you are in, you will have competitors. On one level, competition is bad; but on other levels, it is actually good and healthy for your business to have competition. Governments actively try and outlaw monopolies (i.e. business that have no competition) so it is unlikely that you will be able to create one! Competitors will try and eat into your revenue, take away market share, copy your good ideas, possibly lure away staff and potentially squeeze margins (make you compete on price). Competition and competitors rank highly in reasons why a small business fails. More often than not, this is a result of a lack of understanding about your competitors and not being able to give yourself a clear value proposition or niche from which to operate. The good elements of competition are:

- It ensures that you don't get complacent and keeps you on your toes;
- The more competitors advertising similar products, the greater the overall demand for the products will be;
- A source of information – by monitoring your competition, you will gain insights into your market;
- A source of staff – having people already trained in your industry can be a great benefit;
- Common locations to bring in customers – you will see in some industries e.g. car dealerships, furniture stores,

adventure gear etc, that retail outlets often congregate together. This is an effective way of sharing advertising and giving customers a "destination" location to source the same products and services.

If you are buying a business, often the existing owners will say they have no competition – they are either naïve or lying. Every business has some form of competition and at the very least, you will have similar products that compete for the discretionary dollar of your customers.

When researching and analysing your competitors there are some useful sources:

- Websites
- Customer feedback
- Competitor's advertising
- Contact them or buy from them (ideally anonymously)
- Suppliers

What you really want to know about your competitors are:

- Market share or turnover
- Proximity or location relative to your business
- Ownership structure (private, listed, franchise, etc)
- Size in terms of staff
- Their Value Proposition
- For a Business to Business operation, understanding their key clients (they normally have their logos plastered all over their website) is useful!

The goal with understanding your competitors is not to keep you up at night, worrying about them but using them as a source of information. Where possible, you want to avoid too much competition or making sure that if you are going to take them on, your value proposition is stronger than theirs. If you find that your value proposition is the same then at some point, either you or they will struggle.

Now that you have a list of your competitors, the key is looking at their value propositions and comparing them to yours. If they are too similar, then you have a problem. Unless you are the existing dominant player then you will need to adjust to find opportunities that differentiate your business! When refining your value proposition, it is useful to understand your target market and what their problems are (and how you are solving them) and what their needs are. The more closely your value proposition aligns to your target market, the easier it will be to connect (and grow) with customers.

If we look at the chicken shop the Value Proposition could be:

- Hot fresh healthy roasted chicken – ready when you are;
- Orders completed in under 3 minutes;
- Free range and environmentally sustainable chickens;
- Open convenient hours, easily accessible on the high street with easy nearby parking;
- Great taste, 100% satisfaction guaranteed or your next order free.

The above will hopefully enable them to differentiate themselves and also in this instance, charge a premium price. There may be other chicken shops nearby BUT do they have the same value proposition? They might have the "cheapest chickens" or may not have parking close by. Linking your Target Market to your Value Proposition and aligning this with the actual product/ services you provide, is a virtuous cycle within your business – as each one reinforces the other.

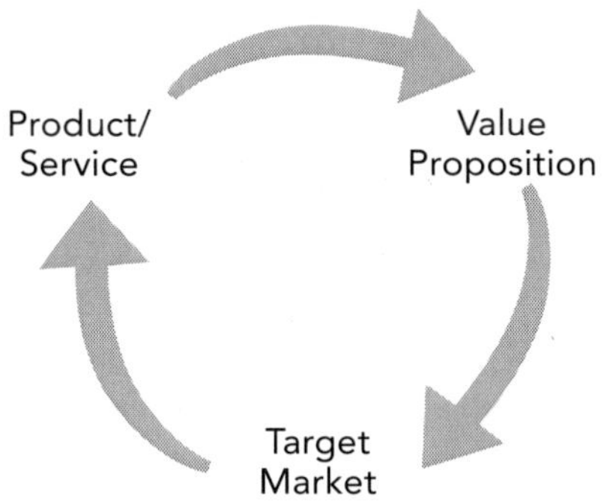

(There is an element in the above of "what comes first – the chicken or the egg…")

Another useful tool when looking at your competition and the Value Proposition is a SWOT analysis i.e. listing the business' (and your ability to execute on the business plan) Strengths Weaknesses Opportunities and Threats. The Strengths and Weaknesses are internally focused and the Opportunities and Threats are externally focused.

Sales and Marketing

The good news is that if you have successfully pulled together your information on your Target Market, have an understanding of your competition and a clearly defined Value Proposition, then sales and marketing should be easy! For your business plan, you need to be able to explain how you intend to drive your sales and what your overall Marketing plan is.

This is all about ***how*** you are going to communicate with your Target Market, grow your Target Market and then convince them to buy your products and services. Existing businesses are a great source of ideas that you can replicate for your own business. Replicating – what your competitors do and what other similar business do to get in front of their customers – is a great way to save you time and effort. No matter what anyone tells you, there is always an unknown element in any form of sales or advertising. It does not always work. The goal for your business is to have a reliable mechanism by which you can generate sales.

On a simplistic level, this is all about cost of acquisition i.e. via what mechanism/ channel, how much does it cost and what level of increased/ sustained sales do you get from it. A lot of this will depend on the type of product that you are dealing with and the maturity of your business. Retail businesses have very different needs to services businesses that target corporates.

The basics of your marketing comes down to the 4 P's:

- Product
- Price
- Position
- Promotion (advertising)

A lot of this is aligning your product(s) and price to your target market, where are you going to sell to them and how are you going to advertise or promote this to them. When buying a business, you should always ask if they have a marketing plan – I suspect that most won't. It is not unusual, even for successful small businesses that have been running for years, to not have a Marketing Plan or a Sales strategy. The reason for this is that in essence, these are already baked into their business. Whether or not they realise this, they have already worked out the key elements to this formula that have been driving their business.

As much as any professional or consultant will tell you, a large amount of marketing and advertising is down to trial and error. The key with taking on board any action or trialling any concept is to be able to measure the results. Ultimately, you should be able to see some result in the top (and bottom) line i.e. an increase in your revenues. Once again, this comes down to cost of acquisition:

- Cost of advertising or promotion, vs
- Increase in number of customers/ increase in revenue

If you take a practical example with "ye olde chicken shoppe" – let us say that you plan to increase some traffic via some facebook or google adword advertising. So you jump onto to their advertising platform, create your ad, set the geographic boundaries as to who will see it. You will set some form of daily/ click budget. Ideally, what you will do initially, is put in place some call to action combined with a tracking mechanism. Best example is a special "one off" code or coupon where someone gets 25% off their first chicken. You might even make it a targeted campaign where the discount applies to say, Tuesday nights – your slowest night. You can then execute the campaign and by tracking the number of coupons or discount codes received, will get an idea of how many people/customers it has attracted.

There are lots of things that you might try – don't be alarmed if some don't work. If they don't work then move on to other ideas and concepts. The key is once you know something doesn't work – don't worry on how much you have spent on it – stop spending money on it and give something else a go.

Business Structure & Operations

Your business structure looks at:

- Legal framework i.e. Sole trader, Company, Partnership etc;
- Ownership – who and via what legal vehicle;
- An organisational chart (assuming you have some staff);
- Roles and responsibilities across your business.

Your Operations looks at:

- Premises;
- Hours of operation/ opening hours;

- Equipment and assets required to run your business;
- Ideally list key processes and activities;
- Suppliers;
- Inventory/stock required;
- Critical personnel, equipment etc.

Even if you are running an online operation, you may consider that things like premises are not relevant but where you host your servers and backups are still relevant.

For your legal structure, you might need advice on the best structure; it is normally best to seek this advice from your accountant or financial planners as 90% of the issues around this are tax related (as well as asset and legal liability protection).

Resourcing plans, be that people or equipment, are very important. You need to understand what you will need to be able to cope with the volumes of activity required. You also need to consider what you might need in terms of growth etc. It is suggested that in line with your organisational chart, you list down the key people in your business:

Job Title	Responsibilities	Years Experience	Skills / Qualifications

Similarly, if you don't yet have the people on board, then include what your hiring requirements are.

Financial Summary

Arguably this is the most important part of the business plan – as you guessed it – it is all about the money! When your business plan is being read by external parties, they will probably spend most of their time looking at the numbers. Certainly when it comes to obtaining finance etc, they will give the greatest consideration to your financial summary. Most people are able chuck a few numbers into a spreadsheet and via a few formulas, make any set of financials say whatever you want it to. The key is that having done the other work around Target Markets, Sales & Marketing, Operations etc, this will help give credibility and confidence in your financial summary.

There are 4 key parts to any set of financials in a business plan:

- Profit and Loss – both historical (for existing businesses) and forecasts;
- Balance Sheet;
- Cashflow;
- Funding requirements.

A lot of books and university courses have been written on accounting and financial models but here is a simplified snapshot of what each one entails.

Profit and Loss looks at your revenue (i.e. Sales), how much it costs to create those sales (i.e. Cost of Goods Sold) and what expenses you have to operate the business. Sales – COGS – Expenses = Profit (hopefully not a Loss). A Profit and Loss is generally structured similar to the table on the next page.

Profit and Loss for Plucky Plucker

	Actuals FY-18	FY-19	Forecast FY-20	FY-21	FY-22
Income/ Sales					
Roasted Chicken	$140,500.00	$145,800.00	*$150,000.00*	*$155,000.00*	*$160,000.00*
Total Income	**$140,500.00**	**$145,800.00**	**$150,000.00**	**$155,000.00**	**$160,000.00**
Less Cost of Sales					
Fresh Chicken	$20,000.00	$20,400.00	*$21,000.00*	*$21,200.00*	*$22,000.00*
Total Cost of Sales	**$20,000.00**	**$20,400.00**	**$21,000.00**	**$21,200.00**	**$22,000.00**
Gross Profit	**$120,500.00**	**$125,400.00**	**$129,000.00**	**$133,800.00**	**$138,000.00**
Plus Other Income					
Interest Income	$0.00	$0.00	*$0.00*	*$0.00*	*$0.00*
Total Other Income	**$0.00**	**$0.00**	**$0.00**	**$0.00**	**$0.00**
Less Operating Expenses					
Advertising	$5,250.00	$6,250.00	*$6,960.00*	*$7,500.00*	*$8,000.00*
Depreciation	$1,280.00	$1,360.00	*$1,380.00*	*$1,450.00*	*$1,500.00*
Electricity	$2,400.00	$2,500.00	*$2,700.00*	*$2,800.00*	*$2,900.00*
General Expenses	$4,500.00	$4,580.00	*$4,560.00*	*$4,700.00*	*$4,800.00*
Insurance	$1,680.00	$1,720.00	*$1,740.00*	*$1,820.00*	*$1,850.00*
Rent	$28,000.00	$29,000.00	*$29,520.00*	*$30,000.00*	*$30,500.00*
Telephone & Internet	$2,200.00	$2,120.00	*$2,160.00*	*$2,300.00*	*$2,350.00*
Wages and Salaries	$60,000.00	$62,000.00	*$63,600.00*	*$66,000.00*	*$68,000.00*
Web Hosting & IT Support	$600.00	$650.00	*$720.00*	*$750.00*	*$800.00*
Total Operating Expenses	**$105,910.00**	**$110,180.00**	**$113,340.00**	**$117,320.00**	**$120,700.00**
Net Profit	**$14,590.00**	**$15,220.00**	**$15,660.00**	**$16,480.00**	**$17,300.00**

What you are showing via the Profit and Loss statement is how much the business is going to be able to earn and what it either has done in the past and what you are predicting it will do it in the future. The rest of the Business Plan is giving substance as to how and why you will be able to achieve these numbers.

The **Balance Sheet** can be a little bit more of a complex concept for someone who has not had any exposure to accounting before. If the profit and loss shows you how much money you have either made in the past or what you hope to make in the future – the balance sheet shows you what you have NOW (or what you had at the date you produced it). It lists all of what you own (assets), what other people owe you (another type of asset), what you owe other people (liabilities). You then add up all your assets, add up all the liabilities then subtract the liabilities from the assets and that shows you the *core monetary value* of your business!

Balance Sheet

Plucky Plucker

	DD-MM-YY
Assets	
Bank	
Business Trans Acct	$2,500.00
Business Savings Account	$15,000.00
Total Bank	**$17,500.00**
Current Assets	
Accounts Receivable	$500.00
Stock on Hand	$3,000.00
Total Current Assets	**$3,500.00**
Fixed Assets	
Computer Equipment	$3,000.00
Less Accumulated Depreciation on Computer Equipment	-$220.00
Fixtures and Fittings	$38,000.00
Less Accumulated Depreciation – Fixtures	-$900.00
Office Equipment	$4,500.00
Less Accumulated Depreciation on Office Equipment	-$400.00
Total Fixed Assets	**$43,980.00**
Total Assets	**$64,980.00**
Liabilities	
Current Liabilities	
Accounts Payable	$1,800.00
GST	$1,280.00
PAYG Withholdings Payable	$1,900.00
Total Current Liabilities	**$4,980.00**
Non-Current Liabilities	
Loan	$50,000.00
Total Non-Current Liabilities	**$50,000.00**
Total Liabilities	**$54,980.00**
Net Assets	**$10,000.00**
Equity	
Current Year Earnings	$12,000.00
Dividends Paid	-$10,000.00
Owner Share Capital	$1,000.00
Retained Earnings	$7,000.00
Total Equity	**$10,000.00**

A balance sheet is something that you will appreciate more as you get used to owning and running a business.

Cashflow and understanding your cashflow is probably one of the most important aspects of running your business. In reality, there is only one way a business can fail – running out of cash. If you still have more cash, you can always do something but once you have no cash and can't get any more, then it is all over red rover! For a lot of small businesses, the profit and loss forecast will basically match your cashflow forecast (particularly if you have a retail business). Where it differs is the timing of when the money actually comes into and out of your bank account. You can get away with having annual profit and loss statements but for cashflow of a small business – monthly is the only option. It is here that you need to understand what cash you require. Lots of small businesses get themselves into trouble when they see the bank account balance shoot up during the peak months – only to realise that a lot of this money is actually required to pay your suppliers, income tax, sales taxes (GST) etc.

A sample of what a Cashflow Forecast might look like:

EXPECTED CASHFLOW [YEAR]	JAN	FEB	MAR	APR	MAY
OPENING BALANCE	**$17,500**	**$21,600**	**$21,200**	**$15,125**	**$17,623**
Cash incoming					
Sales	$15,000	$10,000	$10,000	$15,000	$10,000
Asset sales					
Debtor receipts					
Other income					
Total incoming	**$15,000**	**$10,000**	**$10,000**	**$15,000**	**$10,000**
Cash outgoing					
Stock Purchases (Chicken etc)	$2,000	$1,500	$1,500	$1,750	$1,500
Equipment Purchases					
Advertising	$580	$580	$580	$580	$580
Electricity			$675		
General Expenses	$380	$380	$380	$380	$380
Insurance					
Rent	$2,460	$2,460	$2,460	$2,460	$2,460
Telephone & Internet	$180	$180	$180	$180	$180
Wages and Salaries	$5,300	$5,300	$5,300	$5,300	$5,300
Web Hosting & IT Support					
GST payments				$1,852.50	
Income Tax					
Dividends/ Owner payments			$5,000		
Total outgoing	**$10,900**	**$10,400**	**$16,075**	**$12,503**	**$10,400**
Monthly cash balance	**$4,100**	**-$400**	**-$6,075**	**$2,498**	**-$400**
CLOSING BALANCE	**$21,600**	**$21,200**	**$15,125**	**$17,623**	**$17,223**

CONTINUED...

JUN	JUL	AUG	SEP	OCT	NOV	DEC
$17,223	**$13,688**	**$16,584**	**$16,184**	**$12,509**	**$9,732**	**$9,332**
$10,000	$15,000	$10,000	$15,000	$10,000	$10,000	$25,000
$10,000	**$15,000**	**$10,000**	**$15,000**	**$10,000**	**$10,000**	**$25,000**
$1,500	$1,500	$1,500	$1,750	$1,500	$1,500	$2,000
$580	$580	$580	$580	$580	$580	$580
$675			$675			$675
$380	$380	$380	$380	$380	$380	$380
$1,740						
$2,460	$2,460	$2,460	$2,460	$2,460	$2,460	$2,460
$180	$180	$180	$180	$180	$180	$180
$5,300	$5,300	$5,300	$5,300	$5,300	$5,300	$5,300
$720						
	$1,703.50			$2,377.50		
			$2,350			
			$5,000			$5,000
$13,535	**$12,104**	**$10,400**	**$18,675**	**$12,778**	**$10,400**	**$16,575**
-$3,535	**$2,897**	**-$400**	**-$3,675**	**-$2,778**	**-$400**	**$8,425**
$13,688	**$16,584**	**$16,184**	**$12,509**	**$9,732**	**$9,332**	**$17,757**

Funding requirements are really the net result of the other financials above and it closes the loop on what end ups in the balance sheet and what funding you need to sustain your cashflow forecast. In the example above, we have shown an existing business that is already running. If you were to start off (or buy a business), you would need to be able to determine the total funding requirements that you will need.

- Start up costs or Purchase price of the business;
- Funding costs i.e. interest payments on debt + principal repayments;
- Working Capital (cash) requirements (this is the amount of cash that you need to have in the business to be able to pay your staff and pay your suppliers on time – taking into account seasonal and regular sales fluctuations).

In your financial summary, you need to be able to identify where your funding requirements are going to come from:

- Existing funds that you are putting into the business;
- Equity capital (i.e. selling shares or equity in the business);
- Debts (i.e. loans and other types of financing).

Don't underestimate the importance of your financial statements and summary. Putting it down on a piece of paper doesn't make it real, but not going through this process and not working out what the business looks like financially, is a sure fire way to trouble.

Executive Summary

Surely the executive summary goes at the beginning? Yes, it does. The reason why this is at the end of this chapter is that you need to have worked out all of the above inputs to be able to pull together an Executive Summary. The best way to think of this section is that it is your elevator pitch – enough information and description about the business and how it operates – that you can tell a person in an elevator ride. Ideally you want to cover:

- What is the business;
- What is its Value proposition;
- What Market does it target;
- Where does it sit competitively;
- What are the next 3 years revenue and profit projections;
- If you are seeking funding, then an idea of the amount of funding required for the business.

If your executive summary is going over a page long – I suggest that you cut bits out.

Chapter Summary/Key Takeaways

A business plan is a vital document for any business. The process of pulling it together and understanding all of the elements is actually more important than the document itself. So I would strongly recommend that you don't outsource this function no matter how daunting you find it. By all means get input from others – and if you are not good at wordsmithing, there is nothing wrong in having others physically write it, but you need to own it!

Once you have written your business plan there are likely to be lots of interested parties that will want to read it. What is more important is that this document shouldn't be left to gather dust or become lost in a folder on your computer. A business plan should be viewed as a living document. There is nothing wrong with changing it and updating it as you learn more.

Now that you have the plan – you need to do something with it!

"In preparing for battle I have always found that plans are useless, but planning is indispensable."

—Dwight D. Eisenhower

Chapter Ten

Have You Got Your Ducks Lined Up?

"HELP I need somebody
(Help) not just anybody
(Help) you know I need someone …
Won't you please, please help me,
help me, help me, ooh?"

–JOHN LENNON & PAUL MCCARTNEY

You are getting close now to Owning your own business. How does it feel? If you are like most normal people, you will be a little bit scared and a little bit overwhelmed. Don't be surprised if you are absolutely SH*tting yourself and feel like your head is two feet underwater! This is a good point to take a quick breath (when your head is above water) just before you take the big plunge and make sure you have everything in place. This chapter will look over all those things that you need to have in place. This is not to deter you from progressing but rather you help optimise your chances of success.

Let's look at some of the key categories:

- YOU
- The BIG plan

- Resources
- Money

You

Are you ready? Big question. This is a good time to have a quick read back over the Business Owner boot camp. Think some of the exercises were far-fetched? Absolutely not. The first and foremost thing you need to be ready for is the amount of work and effort you will need to put into making *your* business work. You need to prioritise this – if I had to pick one thing and one thing only then this would be it. If you are not prepared for this then you need to get ready for it! Hard work – your own time and effort is the catch all for everything else that can go wrong. Hopefully you are still passionate and excited about the opportunity ahead. Owning a Business is where you translate your ideas, your hard work, your passion into a growing asset and where **you** reap the rewards of your success. Having something that you are truly passionate about can level mountains, make the impossible seem possible and drive you places you never thought you could achieve!

For you to be ready, you need to check off the following:

- Readiness to work hard!
- Training. Have you undertaken an assessment of your Strengths and Weaknesses? Is there any experience or training that you can get before you start? At the very least, having an understanding of what you are NOT good at will allow you to supplement this with others that have those skills. Having a list of areas for development will also allow you to seek out opportunities to improve your skills and knowledge when they arise.
- Willingness to be flexible and open minded. With a small business, your ability to control the external environment is

basically Nil. You will be buffeted by an unlimited number of external events. Your mindset needs to be open to adapt and change where necessary to cope and take advantage of these events.

- Willingness to learn. Unless this isn't your first rodeo, you will need to be willing to learn lots of new skills and be stretched in all different directions.
- Engaged your friends and family. Have you told everyone what it is you are doing? At some stage along the journey you will need their support and help. Getting their buy in now is a lot easier than when everything is going pear shaped.
- Readiness to work hard! (in case you missed it the first time).

Being personally ready for the challenges that lie ahead is one of the most important things you can do. The best part about this is that it is totally **in your control**!

The Big Plan

In the previous chapter you have developed a couple of plans – the *how* to own your own business plan and also **the** Business Plan. Before you start, it is good to reflect on why you are doing this and what you want to get out of it. Knowing the end goal of owning your own business will heavily influence how you set everything up. What are you after?

- Is this a 5-year money making adventure?
- Is this a business (job) for life?
- Is this a lifestyle play?

The destination you want to achieve should drive how you set things up. For example if the goal is, to buy/build a business then flog it off in x years' time, then you want to create a legal and financial structure that supports this. This would require you to keep everything as clean as possible within the business (i.e.

no personal expenses) or side businesses. You need to be able to neatly partition off what it is you are going to sell. This also means that your decisions about investments should be driven towards that time goal. You may choose to invest more heavily earlier in the piece so that you maximise the business growth and results towards the timeframe of exit.

Your exit plan should be clear from the outset. If you don't start planning when and how you wish to exit right from the beginning, then you will struggle to optimise your results. Small businesses are a highly illiquid investment – so any change in ownership takes time and planning. If your ultimate goal is to have a lifestyle business i.e. one where you end up spending minimal time and effort whilst it generates cashflow to fund your lifestyle, then you need to plan for this. This will ultimately result in you structuring the business via the appropriate staff and process and procedures to make running the business require a minimal level of input. These sorts of goals should be driving your decisions as you start and also run the business.

With the end goal or destination firmly in your mind, you need to review your Business Plan to make sure that it matches.

- Will you achieve the growth required to build the asset up to the required size?
- Do you have enough funds to afford to make the investment necessary for growth or for hiring the calibre of people you need?
- Are some of your competition, also future acquirers of your business?
- If you build the business according to your plan, will it be attractive to another purchaser in x years' time?
- Is the financing enough to see you through to the exit?

- Will organic growth be enough to get you to your destination or will you need to potentially acquire more businesses?

Whilst some of this may seem like counting your chickens before they have hatched, it is not saying that all of this will occur but rather this is what you need to make happen. Given the lumpy and illiquid nature of a small business investment, by not planning ahead you make the probability of ultimate success a lot less. There is also nothing wrong with you having an "external" Business Plan and an "internal" Business Plan. What do I mean by this? Well your *external* business plan is the one that you would provide to banks, maybe even show some staff to get them excited. This presents your aspirations and strategic direction. Your *internal* business plan is the one where you apply a strategic layer about ***your*** exit plan and what your objectives are out of the business. Staff and banks and some advisors don't need to know that you plan to sell the business off in five years!

You need to also match the legal structure and ownership of the business to reflect the ultimate plan. This is where your accountant or legal advisor can give you the right solution – you would let them in on the "internal" business plan – so they can help you structure it correctly.

Finally, is the business that you plan to own – whether you are building it or buying it – does it match your big picture objectives? Your original prioritised Motivation List of what you want to get out of owning your own business – are these being met?

Resources

To make anything happen you need resources! Resources are everything from plant and equipment, to staff, to external consultants. What resources you need, will be highly dependent on what the business is. The rough categories that you will be looking at are:

- Office equipment. This is everything from tables, chairs, computers, telephones, internet access. You will also need office consumables (those you haven't acquired from your previous employer) – stationery, toilet paper...
- Software– spreadsheet, word processer, email, CRM, accounting platform etc
- Premises – where are you going to operate from?
- Premises fitout. Depending on the business, this can range from an entry lounge or a kitchen, through to retail shopfront fitout.
- Equipment and tools. This is the machinery you will need to manufacture your products or make delivering your services easier.
- Vehicles – cars/ vans – depending on the business you operate.
- Insurance – basics like property, theft, fire – through to business interruption – product and professional liability insurance. Directors' insurance?
- Supporting Services. This is the army of highly specialised skills that you will hopefully only need occasionally but you want to have on hand in case you do need them:
    - Lawyer
    - Accountant
    - HR support – may be the lawyer
    - Business Broker
    - Insurance Broker
    - Bank/Financier
    - Real Estate agent

- Suppliers – depending on your business, the relationships and arrangements you have with your suppliers are often key to the success of your business. I always advocate building and maintain good relationships. Contractual agreements are great but a well-run business has a great supply chain with supportive partners.
- Staff – you need to thinking of not only what staff you need from day one, but also what you might need as you grow the business. How long does it take to train staff? What lead time are you likely to face in acquiring additional staff?

Reviewing the list of resources that you require helps you be prepared for what lies ahead. You will also need to review your business plan to make sure that you have accounted for ALL the resources you require both from an execution perspective and also a financial perspective. Have you factored in the cost of acquiring or paying for all the resources that you need? In some businesses, you can make a conscious choice to forgo some resources that you may need. This is normally done on a cost benefit basis or a risk reward basis. The important thing is that you make this choice and understand what you are risking or what the consequences of that are. An example of this is that you may forgo Product liability insurance – if the volume of the products sold is low and the risk level of the product low, it may not be worth it – particularly when you are just starting out. When you have a larger business selling millions of dollars of product, the risk of losing the business may then be worthwhile insuring against that possibility. Another good example is that many small businesses start off being operated from a spare room in your home; in this case, your premises (and a lot of the office equipment) is "borrowed" from your personal life. This may not be ideal but might be very cost effective. Once again as your business grows and has more revenue and customers, to support this, you may upgrade to external premises (and incur the additional rent, fitout, etc).

Money

Probably the most important resource you will need is Money. As you have realised throughout this book, finance – having access to capital or money – is a key theme. This is where you want to pick up that Business Plan, look over your financial forecasts – particularly your cashflow forecast – and ask yourself, "Have I got enough money?"

Money is most easily obtained when you DON'T need it. Banks and Financial Services providers are most keen to provide you money when you don't want it. When the chips are down and you really need it, they will be the least likely to give it to you! If you are still employed, it is so much easier to get a loan or access to credit with a normal employee's salary behind you.

I would certainly recommend that marshalling as much spare capital is one of the best ways of mitigating any risks that might come along with owning and running your own business. This can be everything from lining up some friends or family "just in case". Having some spare capital that you can access will help you to sleep easier at night and relieve the stress and pressure off many a situation. If you are sitting there and facing losing the lot, your options on how to proceed are often limited. External parties that you owe money to will not have you or your businesses' best interests at heart – all they will care about is the best chances of them getting their money/capital back!

A few simple things that you can do:

- Check the limits on your credit cards – can you increase these?
- Have you worked out the maximum that you can borrow up front?
- Apply for any loans or credit card increases when you still have a normal job

- Line up some friends or family for some emergency "lines of credit"

So look over the financials of the business once again. Have some plan B, C and D's as to how, in a pinch, can you get access to extra capital if required. You want to do this when the going is good, not when it has all gone pear shaped!

Chapter Summary/Key Takeaways

Businesses involve lots of moving parts. You want to maximise your chances of success by ensuring you have everything you need – or at least be in the position where you have made a conscious choice to forgo those needs. Run through the checklist below and fill as many gaps as possible!

The checklist

- ❑ Readiness to work hard!
- ❑ Training in place
- ❑ Flexible and open minded
- ❑ A learning mindset
- ❑ Support of friends and family
- ❑ Prioritised Motivation List of why you want to own your own business
- ❑ Your end goal worked out
- ❑ An exit plan/strategy
- ❑ Business plan aligns with your end goals
- ❑ Legal and ownership structure aligned with your end goals
- ❑ Resources aligned with Business Plan
- ❑ Premises
- ❑ Equipment
- ❑ Software
- ❑ Staff
- ❑ Suppliers
- ❑ An updated Business Plan!
- ❑ Enough Money
- ❑ Emergency sources of Money, ready and in place

So now you are ready to roll...

Chapter Eleven
What is Stopping You?

"Just DO IT"
—NIKE

You have made it this far – this either means you have cheated and just flipped to this chapter, you find my writing entertaining or you actually really want to own your own business! I am going to go with the last one. Assuming that you don't already own your own business something must be stopping you. This is invariably self-objections and at the heart of these, are the same set of emotions – fear – doubt – uncertainty. Whilst it is very easy to say, don't be afraid or don't worry – if it was that easy, you would have done it already.

The message from this chapter is that it is ok to be a little bit worried, a bit fearful and a bit stressed about what you are doing. When owning your own business, you need to be on your toes. If there is one clear message that should have by now, it is that owning your own business is hard work. It is not easy. As long as you can handle that, everything else can be put in its place. I have put together a simple process below to help you on your way and get you owning your own business:

1. Understand and overcome your objections

2. Working the plan
3. Get others to help you

Understand and overcome your objections

If you have ever done any sales, then you will understand how important it is to overcome objections. Just as in sales, you will need to get to the heart of your own objections and sell yourself as to how they can be overcome. Some will be genuine impediments that you will need to come up with solutions for, but many others will be mental blocks that are getting in your way of making this a reality. Let's explore some:

- **Not enough Money or can't afford to**. Certainly not having enough money or capital available can stifle a business and increase the risks. If you go back to chapter Eight and re-read it, you will see that there are lots of avenues to obtain the money that you need to run a business. Also if funds are tight, you may want to see how you can kick start the business in your part time – just so that you can get going, prove the concept and maybe even supplement your existing income. Once something is actually running, you will find obtaining finance for it, easier. Similarly, maybe rather than start something from scratch, you can investigate purchasing an existing business, which once again will be easier to obtain finance for. There are always sources of capital out there. It just depends on the price you are willing to pay to obtain that capital.
- **Why would I give up a great job to risk it all on owning a business?** I hear this all the time. Conceptually being a salaried employee is a lot less risky (and requires less work). If you are in that position, that you have a well- paid job and that you enjoy, you are probably good at it. I suspect that there is something more that you are after. It could be financially driven or it could be that you are passionate about something else. Go back and look at your Motivation List. I am sure that there are number of

things that are driving you to own your own business. Compare the Motivation List to your current job – does it tick all the boxes? I doubt it. Nothing ventured – nothing gained! If you are really (really) worried about moving on from your job, you can always give yourself a parachute – take six months leave without pay to give this a go. If your employer won't give it to you then they probably don't value you that much – in which case, it is a good time to leave anyway. IF you are good at your job and valued by your employer, then they are more than likely going to be willing to take you back if things don't work out. It is very rare that an employer won't value the skills and experiences that you will gain from owning your own business. They may not be happy that you want to leave and give it a go but they should respect your drive and ambition in having a go!

- **It is going to be hard work**. Yes, it is. I am glad you have come to that conclusion. But consider this – what do you consider work? Owning a small business consumes vast amounts of time – but is it really work? If you are doing something you really want to do, it is not really "work", it will hopefully be rewarding and fun. You are much better off spending 80 hours a week on something that gives you a sense of satisfaction and with you reaping the rewards, than 40 hours of dreary soul sucking work! Hard work in your own business = success, rewards and satisfaction.
- **There are no businesses for sale in the industry I want**. I certainly wouldn't advocate just buying any business at any price. The good news is that opportunities to buy businesses come along frequently. You need to make sure that you have carefully understood what and why you have picked a particular industry or business that you want to own. Most people, when you get down to it, are not that passionate about a specific industry but are more interested in the qualities of that sort of business. If you adjust the way

you look at the qualities of the business i.e. not in terms of industry but in terms of the features of that business, you may open up a much larger range of possibilities. If you are deeply passionate about something then yes, pursue that passion. Have you approached other existing businesses about maybe, buying them? You can use a broker to do this or you can directly approach them. Most business owners will at least give it some thought. Through this process, you are at the very least likely to learn something. Another way might be to find a complimentary business that is for sale – does it service the same customer? Does it have similar products? Similar suppliers? Otherwise if there is only one thing you want to do, then the other option may be just to start up your own business. Opportunities are out there – you just need to hunt them down!

- **My business model doesn't stack up**. That is a bit of a problem. If the business model won't work (i.e. can't make enough money) then you need to change it! You might need to look at either a lower cost of supply, selling a premium product, expanding the area that you can service so as to expand the target market. If the product is very niche, then you may need to supplement it with other products to give you the volume and turnover you need to sustain the business. This is where calling in some professional help might be good. There are any number of business consultants out there – try and pick one that has real industry experience in the type of business you are trying to create. Simple answer is – if the business model doesn't work – change it so that it does!
- **I'll just wait until I get my bonus**. There are always reasons for you to stop or wait until later to own your own business. You might be part of an industry where bonuses or some other events like long service leave – can be a significant financial shot in the arm. So whilst I am not suggesting that

you leave "free" money on the table – consider the cost of waiting? If you have found a great opportunity, then grab it. Owning your own business is about a 3-5-10 year journey. Hopefully the financial returns that you will ultimately, one day get, will far out way any that you are leaving behind. Organisations are very clever about the ways they look to retain staff or create incentives to stay, but they are not there to help you own your own business! Look at the bigger picture and just do it.

- **I might fail**. Probably the biggest de-motivator for people looking to own their own business – the fear of failure. The statistics about business failures are awful. Could you fail – absolutely. That is not a reason to let it stop you. The rewards for owning your own successful business can be huge. Even beyond the financial outcomes, the amount you will learn and the experiences you will gain will make you a more valuable person. Without risk there is little chance of reward. Look at it this way – are you more a failure by not giving something a go, than having given it a go and not succeeded? Most great entrepreneurs have had a failure (or two or more) in their careers. Failure is where you learn the best lessons. Embrace the fact that yes, you may not create a financial success, but take with that the hard lessons learned – so that next time you can do it even better!
- You may have other objections that are direct and personal to you. Write them down and create a pros vs cons. For every con that you come up with, find an opportunity or strength that you can counter it with. You will find that sometimes your biggest concerns highlight some of your best opportunities! Once you look at these in the cold light of day, a lot of concerns will be minor compared to the opportunity that lies ahead of you.

Working the plan

Do you recall Project OMOB (Own My Own Business) from chapter Five? Well assuming that you are not reading this book on your leisurely time off from running a business, then that plan is still in play. Pull it out and dust it off. If you don't have a target date or a key milestone in there to "Start running my own business", then you need to put one in there.

Go through the list of tasks that you have laid down for yourself (and others) – what is still outstanding? Owning your own business rarely happens overnight so you need to remain committed and focused to get it done. Having a plan with a set of tasks in front of you helps to make it real. You can then see what you need to get done. It may seem large daunting and overwhelming but by breaking it down into smaller components, you can tick these off one by one. If the plan doesn't have all of these – update it – make it relevant.

If you haven't already got the drift, a plan is only useful if you work to it. You don't have to be constrained in a rigid fashion if the plan had omission or inaccuracies – you can change and update it. To help you get your own business up and running here are some tasks you want to be tracking towards:

ID	What	How Much	When	Who
1	Create Project OMOB plan	1 plan	1st Jul	Me
	Confirm financial capacity i.e. get finances in place	X Dollars	20th Jul	Me
	Select chosen business	Target business criteria	1st Aug	Me
	Create the Business Plan	1 Business Plan	30th Aug	Me
	Create Exit Strategy	1 Exit Strategy	15th Sep	Me
	Create Legal Structure	1 Structure	30th Sep	Me

	Confirm Resources are in place	1 Resource list	10th Oct	Me
	Execute contracts	1 Lease 1 Contract for sale …	15th Oct	Me
99	Start running my own business	1 Business	1st Nov	Me

There will be many, many other tasks that will be on your Project OMOB schedule. Print it out – stick it on you wall. Cross off and update the plan's schedule as you progress. Don't get despondent if not everything is running according to your schedule – try, wherever possible, NOT to move your end target date but be realistic. The most important thing is to continue to make progress no matter how slowly you are going. There will always be things outside your control. You might be buying a business and the purchase might fall through or during due diligence, you might find some red flags that stop you from buying the business. Just because you have an end date in mind doesn't mean that you should arbitrarily pick or start a business, just to meet that date. Once you own a business you can't just stop; it is a multi-year commitment.

Work the plan – keep it updated and constantly strive to get the next task on the list actioned and completed!

Getting others to help

Rarely is a successful business a solo affair. Along the way, you will need the help of many people. Some of these will be paid consultants – accountants, lawyers, business brokers, etc. Others will be paid employees – your staff. Hopefully there will also be others, such as friends and family, that will join you in some way along the journey.

If you are genuinely serious about owning your own business, then you need put a stake in the ground and commit to this goal. One of the best ways to do this is to tell or announce this to you friends and family. This serves two very important purposes.

The first of these purposes is that it is a call for help. You might have a good idea about the strengths and weaknesses of those that you know – but you might be surprised. The friends and family that you talk to are likely to either have some capabilities that you were not aware of or likely, would know some people that might be able to help you. The type of help that you can/will get, is lots of advice. Some of this may be complete dribble but you are also likely to come across all sorts of viewpoints that you haven't thought of or considered. In my experience, you will be flooded with lots of ideas about how you can start or grow the sort of business that you are looking at. Once again, a lot of these will be useless BUT amongst these will be golden opportunities. The ones that are likely to be useful will be tangible ones e.g. I can introduce you to the CEO of xyz who might want to use your services. "Ideas" are generally free and plentiful – contacts and introductions are golden! The other type of help that you may get from them is possibly even more important – financial. By letting them know of your intentions, you give them fair warning. Hopefully out of this, you may get some unsolicited offers for some money or you may not. Any offers should be gratefully considered and like any contact, you should keep these "warm" throughout the process.

The second purpose is that it makes your intention real and public. Once you have told someone that you are going to do or try something, you are now on the hook to follow through with what you intend to do. Friends and Family are a great safe starting point about going public with what you are doing. You can ask them to keep it confidential, if you don't want others such as your employer to know. You do need to be realistic however, in that, even the most trustworthy of friends can leak information and gossip unintentionally (and also intentionally). The key here is that by telling them, you now have an army of supporters that will, on occasion, follow you up and ask you how you are progressing. This is a great way to help keep you honest and on track. I suggest that when you tell them, you give them a snippet of your OMOB Plan i.e. a few key tasks and dates that you are targeting towards.

There is also a side benefit in that any form of communication is good – and your friends and family should appreciate that you are keeping them in the loop! No one ever complains about not being surprised.

Chapter Summary/Key Takeaways

To get there and really own your own business, you need to remain committed and focused. The great news is that focus and commitment are key attributes in being successful in running a business! It is up to **you** to make this all happen. Throughout the chapter, we explored a number of ways to "Just do it":

- Overcoming objections – face your fears and concerns; understand and embrace these as opportunities or weaknesses that you need to supplement with either help or self- improvement;
- Have a plan – and most important – a timeline/ schedule in place. Tick off each task one at a time; keep that end goal and date in focus;
- Enrol others to help. Make it real. Make it public. With supporters behind you, the passage forward will be easier.

Hopefully you are pumped up with the strains of "Eye of the Tiger" coursing through your brain. Now then, let's explore whether or not you should go it alone...

Chapter Twelve
Should I go it Alone?

"If you want to go fast, go alone.
If you want to go far, go together."
—African Proverb

Owning your own business is a big deal. It requires lots of work and effort to make it a success. It is rare that a business will be a long term success, riding off the back of a single individual. In fact, if you want to build an asset that will be valuable to others, you need to have a business (at least when you come to exit) that has capable staff working in it. It is also very rare that an individual will have such a broad range of skills and capabilities that they can do it all themselves. So should you be looking to buy (or start) a business with a partner?

Let's be clear that what we are talking about here is not just the "ownership" side but also the day to day running and managing of the business. In this instance, we will differentiate between a part owner that is merely there for helping to provide finance, or a husband and wife team who jointly "own" a business, but the other one doesn't work in it.

If you are able to find a business partner involved that has complementary skills (access to funding), it can be a powerful force in running and growing a business. The old saying "two heads are better than one" certainly applies. It is not necessarily all smooth sailing and many small businesses have fallen apart due to conflict between owners/ management.

Owning and running a business with another person is almost as important a decision as owning your own business. There are a few key items that you need to consider:

- Why do you need or want a business partner?
- What should you look for and/or look out for in a business partner?
- Putting in place a written agreement
- What do you do when it all goes to sh*t?

Why have a business partner?

There are lots of drivers to have a business partner when owning a small business. The key factors will differ depending on your situation but for most, the drivers will be:

- Access to additional funds and finance. Particularly if you are looking at buying an existing business you may find that the initial funds that you require may be more than what you can finance on your own. Jointly purchasing a business is a valid way of obtaining those additional funds. You need to consider carefully about whether they are a business partner from a funding/ownership perspective only or also part of the day to day running and decision making within the business.
- Acquiring additional skills and capabilities. Early on in the book, it was suggested that you get feedback on what your strengths and weaknesses are. Most people will be stronger in particular areas than others. Having a weakness is fine as long as you understand what it is and you can put in place compensatory resources to overcome these. Bringing on board a business partner can be a great way to obtain access to a great skill set. Certainly for one of my recent business endeavours, I partnered up with another person. I had very

strong organisational and customer service skills and my partner had a strong background in business development and sales! If this is the driving reason for bringing on board a business partner – just like hiring a new employee – you have to vet and check that what they purport their skills to be, is actually real. This is best achieved by some reference checks or even just looking at the practical results that they have achieved at their previous business or places of work.

- Confidence. If this is the first time you are owning your own business, it can be daunting and frightening. Not doing this on your own is a great way to potentially reduce the risk and give you more confidence. This is particularly helpful if you are not sure, of your own capabilities or of your underlying knowledge of the business field that you are going to operate in. Having someone else by your side as you face the challenges of owning your own business can be very comforting. It also means that you are not a single point of failure e.g. what happens if there is a family emergency, you get sick, etc?
- Accountability and focus. Have you ever noticed that a bicycle peloton will catch a lone rider? Some of this is impact of wind resistance but a large part is, that the group drags you along and keeps you moving forward – constantly. Having a business partner can be like that for a small business i.e. together, it is easier for you to push forward than you facing all the resistance on your own. Everyone will have a bad or a down day every so often. Having someone else in your corner pushing you along can be very helpful in those occasions. Also when someone else is holding you accountable for your actions, you are more likely to focus on delivering on your required outcomes. There can also be some level of friendly rivalry where you may seek to outdo each other. This is normally in the area of sales but can also easily apply for any set of targets you choose to pursue.

- Operating solo is just hard to do. Ultimately you know that to have a business grow and succeed it is not the endeavour of just one individual. As an owner, your drive and passion will always exceed even the most motivated of employees. The fact that you are the ultimate financial beneficiary of the results of the business, drives you harder than anyone else. So if that works for one owner then why not one or more?

There are potentially many more drivers that make you seek or choose to join others in a business partnership in owning your own business. It is not always all smooth sailing with having a business partner. There are many potential downsides as well.

The first consideration you need to look at is your prioritised Motivation List in owning your own business. If your motivations revolve around having control or being in charge, then any act that removes or dilutes your ability to run the show, can impact this. Having a business partner, even one that own "less" of the business than you, can reduce this level of control. When you have a business partner – no matter what you think – they will still have a seat at the table and will need to be treated as some form of equal. So if the control aspects and being master of your own destiny are important to you, then tread very carefully in bringing on board a business partner.

The other key consideration is the monetary side of things. Whatever amount of Equity or Ownership you share with another, it will have an impact on the monetary outputs of the business. When you own your own business, you are likely to make money in 4 basic ways:

- Salary paid to you from the business;
- Interest payments paid to you in the instance that you have "loaned" the business funds;

- Dividends paid to you from the profits of the business;
- The proceeds from the ultimate sale of the business.

By having a business partner, all the above can be impacted. Any salary paid to you will need to be agreed with the business partner (and likewise, any salary that they get paid). If there are loans into the business, then they are likely to be from both parties. Dividends are normally paid out based on the ownership of the business e.g. if you own 75% you get 75% of the dividends. When you are the sole owner of the business, you would get 100% of the dividends i.e. the payout of the profits. Finally, on the sale of the business, the proceeds are similarly split by ownership. Once someone obtains an ownership in the business, you can't just take that away from them – it is theirs into perpetuity! The key message here is that, if the financial outcomes are a key motivator, then any split in ownership splits the return on the investment of your capital and your time. If you have dreams of having a business that makes you $100k per year, then if you have a 50% partner, you need to buy/build/grow a business that makes $200k per year! It is a lot easier to manage and run a business that is making $100k in profit per annum, than one that is making $200k. Every incremental uptick in size makes it harder and more time consuming to manage! The other way to think of it is – the benefit in having a 50% partner needs to be more than double what they bring to the table, as every $ profit you make will be halved. 1+1 needs to equal 3!

What makes a good business partner?

You may or may not get a choice in who ends up as your business partner. A lot will depend on whether or not it is you approaching them or them approaching you! Either way, you need to make an assessment as to whether or not they will make a good business partner. The first thing to consider is what is driving you to seek out a business partner – is it, access to money; is it, seeking certain skills that you are missing; is it that you just need help? Understanding the *why* is critical in determining whether or not you have the right person. If it is not access to money that is driving the partnership, you should explore the possibility if could you just have them as an employee or possibly an employee with some equity upside if they help drive success and deliver on results. The benefit of just having someone as an employee rather than a joint owner in a business is that, if things don't turn out well – either the business doesn't perform or they don't perform – the ability to get rid of them is a lot easier.

A lot of people will naturally tend towards seeking out friends when they go looking for a business partner. This can work out very well. It can tick lots of boxes BUT are they actually fulfilling what you need a business partner for? The other element is that owning and running a small business can place unwanted strain and external pressures on you and any relationships that you have. It can be terrible facing the financial strain of a failed business but it can be even worse if you face the added strain of losing an important friendship at the same time. When you are considering going into business with someone you know, be even more critical of people that you are already friends with – you have more to lose if you get it wrong!

The reason why people often head towards friends is that they do cover off many of the key aspects that you want in a Business Partner. Let's run through these now:

- **Do they have the skills you need?** The natural inclination in life is to spend time with people who are like you. If you like the same things, think the same way, are good at the same things then you are more likely to gravitate towards each other. The challenge that you have in a business is that if you have the same or similar skill set, then you are not enhancing the value package that having a business partner can bring. Ideally you need a business partner that has skills that are *different* to what you have. When I say skills, it is also the attributes that you bring to the table. Are you detail oriented? Are you a people person? Are you a big picture person? Are you extroverted? Are you introverted? For example, if you are both detailed- oriented people, that is great as you will probably get along and love getting into the minutia of the business but what about the big picture? Who is going to bring the vision and the strategy to the business? Go back to your strengths and weaknesses and seek out business partners that have strengths where you have weaknesses and vice versa.

- **Can you trust them (and can they trust you)?** Trust is vitally important in a business partnership. You don't have time to spend trying to run a business and not have absolute trust and faith in your business partner. You can and should put in appropriate processes – particularly about money handling – so the temptation never gets too great. It is also prudent to have checks and balances in place to make sure that nothing is going awry but if you get to the point where you feel the need to spy on or monitor the ins and outs of what your business partner is doing, either the relationship has been trashed or you have picked the wrong person! You need to think of it in the context of, if you were absent from the business for say, a month, you want to be able to trust your business partner explicitly to be able to do the right thing over that sort of time frame. This does not mean that they have all the skills to run it on their own but that you trust that they would do the right thing. Similarly, you need to make sure that they trust you. Just as damaging to the business is if they feel the need to spend a great deal of time checking up on what *you* are doing. If they don't have a similar level of trust in you, then it won't work very well.

- **Do they share the same values?** Values influence the core of everything that you do. Whilst in the first point you don't want a carbon copy to be your business partner, you need to at least share a lot of common values. With common values, it will help shape what you do, reinforce the trust between you and also remove future points of conflict between you. When you sit down and have the conversation about being business partners, it is wise to document and share your values. Some partners even express these as part of their partnership agreement.
- **Do you get on well with them?** One of the common themes throughout this book is that owning your own business takes a lot of time and effort. Given that you are likely to be spending a LOT of time with them, if you don't or can't get on well with them – unless there is an amazingly compelling reason – then don't have a business partnership with them. Have you ever had to work with someone you really don't like? It makes the working day a chore and an unpleasant experience. The last thing you want is to trap yourself into owning a business that you will dread and hate working in every day. Nicolas Cole in inc.com puts it in these terms – "If you can't see yourself going on vacation with this person, then don't do it". Probably sage advice!
- **Can you communicate openly?** To run a business, you have to be real about what is going on. You can't afford to have poor communication hold back what you are doing. You need to have a business partner that you can talk openly and honestly with. There will be times when there are real challenges and issues that the business will have to face. This could be anything from running out of cash, to having to sack a staff member, to the loss of a major account. You may even need to have the hard conversation with them about their own performance (and vice versa). If you can't have these sorts of

conversations, then you need to seek out another business partner. Typically, the problems will arise with someone (and it might be you) that is either overly passive aggressive or overly openly aggressive. These sorts of behaviours drive avoidance in having the conversations that need to be had.

- **Are their motivations complementary to yours?** You are looking to own your own business for a set of reasons. If your business partner doesn't have similar or at least, a complementary set of reasons, then it probably won't work. A good example might be that you want to achieve a certain level of profitability and they might want life work balance. You may want control and like running the show and on the flip side, they may not want the stress of being in charge. Whilst these motivations are different they are actually complimentary. It is sometimes harder when your motivations are exactly the same! Understand what is motivating them to get into this business partnership (and similarly help them to understand what is motivating you). I would suggest that you openly share your Motivation List with any prospective business partner.
- **Is the vision the same?** What are you hoping to get out of the business? Does this match what your business partner is seeking to achieve? A simple example is that they might be happy to run the business as a cash cow – seeking a well-funded lifestyle – whereas you might be seeking to grow the business and achieve greater financial results. Difference in your vision for the business will create points of friction. If you are not both headed in the same direction, it is unlikely that both or either of you will get there.

You will be spending a great deal of time with a business partner. They don't have to be your best friend but it has to be someone that you can collaboratively work with and ideally enjoy spending time with. They also need to bring something to the table that you don't have. That may be as simple as time, money or some specialised skills.

Written partnership agreement

Regardless of who you bring on board as a business partner, there is one thing you **absolutely must do** and that is to have a written partnership agreement. This needs to be some form of a legally binding document. This may take the form of an actual partnership agreement or a shareholders' agreement or just a contract between the partners.

Key items that the agreement needs to cover are:

- Salary or payment to be made to the partners;
- How changes to salary will be agreed;
- What are the expected ours of work;
- Ideally it should cover a statement of the vision that you are trying to achieve with the business;
- How decisions regarding investment and expenditure will occur;
- How one or both parties can terminate the agreement i.e. the partnership;
- A mechanism for mediation if the relationship turns sour!

Other more finite items that may also be covered include the death of a partner, what happens if a partner ceases to work in the business, what happens if a partner is not performing etc. There is no doubt that pulling together such a written agreement is likely to create a point of friction. This is good – if you can't work out a written agreement together before you start, then you have no chance of being able to successfully run a business. Remember that this sort of agreement is there to protect both parties but also to protect the asset that you are investing your money and time in. Ideally you will haggle and argue over the contents and wording, but once it is done you can put it in the cupboard and forget about its contents. You know that once you start going back to your legal partnership agreement to check clauses, then you know the relationship is in trouble!

Breakdown of partnerships

You only have to look at the divorce rates to see that even the most promising of partnerships can end in tears. There is no guarantee that who you get into business with can sustain a long term working relationship. If they are your employees, then (subject to local laws) you can always sack them. Once someone owns a part of the business, they own part of the business. You can't just get rid of them that easily. The best way to avoid a breakdown in a partnership is to have a partnership with the right person; someone that you can work with and maintain a professional relationship through the easy and the hard times.

The first signs with a breakdown in the partnership is when you recognise that things are not working. Certainly my advice is that if the partnership is causing you grief and upsetting your satisfaction with owning a business, you need to call out what is going on and have that hard conversation with your business partner. This doesn't mean that you need to get aggressive or demanding but half the battle with partnership breakdowns is the communication. At least if you have the conversation with them, you can make sure that they are aware of what you are feeling (and more often than not, a partnership breakdown is emotionally driven) and what the issues are. You might be surprised that they may not realise that there is a problem. Let us have a look at some of the common reasons why it might breakdown:

- Unequal workload or effort being put into the business i.e. one party is not working as hard as the other
- Unequal delivery of success

- Poor decision making
- Disruptive behaviour
- Personality conflicts
- Dishonest or misleading behaviour
- Theft or illegal actions
- The business is failing...

The list can go on and on, but a lot of them will have elements of the above. It normally comes about from one party feeling that the other isn't contributing as much to the success of the business. Rarely does someone complain that their business partner is working too hard or being too successful!

Once you have identified the problems and communicated to the other party about the issues, then the best course of action is to get a **written agreement** as to what actions need to be taken to resolve this. If you can't agree then it is a sign of more difficult things to come. The actions need to be fair and reasonable otherwise you are just setting the other party up for failure – which will trigger more arguments.

If you can't resolve the issue directly together, then it is time to bring in adult supervision and get an independent third party to help try and resolve the differences. This is important as it helps to take the emotion out of the process and gives an independent sounding board. You never know it might actually be *you* that is being too demanding and unreasonable on your business partner. This may result in you resetting your expectations.

So if you try all of the above and it still isn't working out then it may be time to terminate the agreement! This is where it becomes really really really important that you have a **Termination Clause** in your written partnership agreement. The only time to negotiate a termination is at the beginning when everything is all rosy in the partnership. Termination agreements are normally quite punitive i.e. the person enacting the termination has an uphill battle to remove the other party. This is sensibly the case, otherwise parties would terminate when nothing is wrong just to make a quick $!

The termination agreement will normally involve one or the other party buying out the other – because that is what it is all about – ownership and control. This will invariably cover:

- Under what conditions you can exercise the right to terminate;
- A way to value the business;
- The time frame under which a termination can occur.

A mechanism that I personally like and is quite effective, is the Buyout or be Bought out. In this mechanism you set a value of the business (this is normally a bit above market). The example would be if you both bought into the business at say a multiple of 3.0 x EBITDA, then in this process the value would be 3.5x EBITDA i.e. there is a 0.5x EBITDA premium. It is not recommended to set the value lower as the person being bought out would be harshly dealt with. The process works in that the initiating party issues the right to terminate – at this point the OTHER party has the right to buy the Initiating party's shares at the nominated value. They would be given a timeframe of say, one month to do so, otherwise the Initiating party can then proceed to buy the other party out at the nominated value.

The above mechanism is fair as it gives the other party the chance to own the business, if they choose not to proceed, then at least they can get a premium to what the market is likely to value the business at. If the business is doing well then this is great – if the business is doing poorly then they may suffer a loss (in which case there is often a clause that values the business at the higher of the say 3.5 EBTIDA value or the original purchase price/value).

The key with all of the above is working out the termination mechanism at the beginning and making sure that it is written down and signed by all relevant parties!

Chapter Summary/Key Takeaways

Owning a business with other people can be a great way to improve your chances of success, de-risk an acquisition and bring on board much needed skills and capability. If you choose to do so:

1. Make sure it aligns with your motivations in owning your own business
2. Make sure you get on well with them
3. Put in place a written agreement!
4. Make sure it is clear in that written agreement how the partnership can be terminated.

Whether or not you own a business with another person – you will still need to run the business.

Chapter Thirteen
How do I Run a Business?

"Starting a successful business is not tricky. Starting a successful business does not require above average intelligence. Starting a successful business ***does*** *require having a pig-headed, purpose-driven tenacity about achieving your life goals and fulfilling your life's vision through providing products and services that offer uncompromising quality in a scalable and duplicatable way."*

CLAY CLARK, THE WHEEL OF WEALTH

Without a doubt everything that has come before has been about getting you to the starting line! The real work of owning your own business starts the day you open your doors and start servicing customers or going out there to bring in new customers. This book is about that journey to get you to the starting line. It would however, be a little bit unfair of me just to leave you with that. This chapter will touch on a few concepts to help keep you going past the starting line.

You never stop learning

When you start with your business you will not know everything. When one day you hang up your boots and retire from owning your own business you still won't know everything. Being a business owner you need to accept this but most importantly, you need to build into your business the ability for YOU to keep on learning. Find what works best for you to learn and gather new information – do you learn by reading? do you learn by doing? do you learn by listening? do you learn better by visual aids and movement? Hopefully you can learn by all of the above methods but chances are that one will be more effective than the others. Find out which one that is and use it.

To give an example, let's say that you learn better by reading. As part of running your own business you should make time (ha!) to continue to read more and more about how to run a business. Start building a list of books to read. Ask other business owners what books that they have found to be helpful. Even if you are only knocking off a chapter or two a week, you need to build in that focus on learning more and improving. Not all books will be helpful; some might be full of garbage suggestions (not this one)! You need to be able to pick and choose what will work best for you.

Reading and books are easy sources but depending on your learning style there are other ways – the key is making a list of content/ actions that you should be taking and spending some time to work your way through that list. You should also be constantly adding to this list as well.

- Learning by reading. Create a list of books and reference material to read. Try and keep the list in the order of interest / applicability to what you are currently doing.
- Learning by listening. Create a list of seminars, presentations, podcasts – useful radio segments. You can pre-record these in your own time. Use potential downtime like when driving in a car to listen to these items of content. You can even get audio books.
- Learning by visuals. Create a list of videos, TV shows, you tube clips that have topics of interest. Ideally these will be pre-recorded so that you can watch these in your "leisure" time.

- Learning by doing. Create a list of skills or concepts that you need/ want to learn. Either find people to show you or teach you or try it out yourself. Learning by doing people will often use other content to get them started e.g. books or you tube videos. They read or watch them but really need to get their hands dirty to "learn" and understand something.

Most of your learning will probably happen outside of your "normal" business hours. Unless you want your staff to do the same, it is not a good look to have the Boss sitting there for hours on end reading or watching you tube clips. Your employees will take this as a message that it is ok for them to do likewise.

Working *ON* your business, not in it

I am not sure if you have heard this phrase before – but it will be critical in enabling you to own a business rather than just owning a job. What do we mean by this phrase? Well it sounds simple but it is often pretty hard to execute. It is really the difference between being the leader or manager of a business or the day to day worker. This is the difference between fulfilling your role as the owner of the business vs fulfilling your role doing work in the business. Let's take some examples using our much loved Plucky Plucker Chook shop.

A customer is waiting for service at the counter

Working **in** your business: You rush over to serve the customer to make sure that they get the level of service that they would expect from your business.

Working **on** your business: You have hired and trained your staff correctly so that they will notice the customer and deliver the service you would expect them to provide.

The chicken needs to be cooked just right

Working **in** your business: You get to work 2 hours early to make sure that the chicken is placed in the cooker and set up correctly. You do this as this is the only way to guarantee that the chicken is cooked to perfection.

Working **on** your business: The instruction and operations are clear with step by step guides as to how to set up the chickens and the cooker to produce the prefect chook. Processes and systems are in place to check and ensure that it is done correctly. You thank and reward your staff for doing it right.

Handing out promotional flyers for discounts during the early week slow periods

Working **in** your business: You walk up and down the neighbouring streets handing out the flyers that you printed on your printer late last night. Offering 20% organically grown cooked chickens on Monday and Tuesdays.

Working **on** your business: You speak to your customers and understand the demographics and needs of your customer – the working, time poor parent! On slow Mondays and Tuesdays, you send a staff member with a trolley of excess freshly cooked packaged chooks along with pre-packed salads at 4:45 each day down to the nearby office blocks – letting the aroma of cooked chicken waft into the offices – and sell what you have at a premium.

A staff member isn't doing their job properly leaving a messy dining area

Working **in** your business: You grab the dust pan and broom, wipers and cleaning fluids. I t just won't be cleaned right and to your satisfaction unless you do it yourself. It is so hard to find good employees these days. It's just too hard to train them.

Working **on** your business: You check the chart on the wall – it says that today the responsible person for cleaning is EmployeeX You find EmployeeX and show the results of poor work in cleaning. You explain that at Plucky Plucker, your customers expect good clean wholesome food – a dirty dining area doesn't reflect that. Does EmployeeX want the customers and fellow staff members to know that he/she can't keep the area clean? The wall on the chart shows that customers rate the dining area as being 5 star clean. Does EmployeeX want to be the person responsible for seeing that drop to only being 4 star or even 3 star clean. You put in place the motivations for staff to do the right thing.

If you just purely want to work in your business, then you are probably better off just having a job. You will struggle to build up a working viable asset if all you ever do is work in your business. Michael Gerber, of the E-Myth series of books, says it best:

"Think of your business as anything but a job!

Go to work on your business rather than in it, and ask yourself the following questions:

How can I get my business to work, but without me?

How can I get my people to work, but without my constant interference?

How can I systematize my business in such a way that it could be replicated 5,000 times, so that the 5000th unit would run as smoothly as the first?

How can I own my business, and still be free of it?

How can I spend my time doing the work I love to so rather than the work I have to do?"

Start and End with the Customer

As much as owning your own business is about you and your own personal journey – if you don't have customers, then you won't have a successful business! Your business needs to be focused around what your customers need from the business and how you will deliver it. Not all businesses need to be the paragon of exceptional service – and what is good service to one customer may be bad service to another. You need to understand what it is *your* customers need and expect.

A small business can compete incredibly effectively against larger better funded competitors if they pick the right niche and provide the right type of service for it. This may be a combination of price, location, timing, availability, speed of service etc. Large competitors often need to provide a cost effective one size fits all strategy that may not work for all customers.

So how do you work this out? Talking to your customers, obtaining feedback and listening are great ways. The best way though, is by measuring and observing what customers *actually* do. Sometimes people don't know why they pick a certain product over another, but they do. By measuring and seeing what customers are actually doing is the best way to see what customers really want. The more you are able to measure and track the better the information – and facts – you will get. This allows you to learn and draw conclusions. It also allows you to then ask the right questions from your customers, to seek validation and further understanding.

If this is not a skill of yours, there are many companies that you can easily spend large amounts of money having them pull together this data for you. You can also look around and see what works for competitors; you might even ask a departing customer from one of your competitors, why they buy from them instead of your own business. You may not like some of the answers but it is better to know! You can also look overseas to see what non-competing firms are doing and how they are being successful. There can always be local cultural nuances that apply but you will be amazed at what insights you might be able to gain. When running your own business, it doesn't matter who came up with an idea first. Often it can be better to let others experiment and then only follow once they have found a winning formula. They say imitation is the sincerest form of flattery. For a small business, the execution of ideas is ten times more valuable than the idea itself!

A final note on this point about the importance of your customers – not only are they the source of your revenue and profit but they can also be the source of great satisfaction. Having truly appreciative and thankful clients can almost be more rewarding than the monetary aspects. In those dim dark hours when things don't seem to be going right, being able to remind yourself of the positive feedback that you get from customers can make all the difference. By following up and asking your customers about how they found your product and services, not only gains you some insights but can also provide some amazingly motivating feedback and comments. Try it and give it a go. When you do get positive feedback, make sure that you share it with your staff as well. Nothing motivates more than positive feedback from your customers.

Chapter Summary/Key Takeaways

Clearly through this chapter I haven't gone into the full details about how you should run a business. There are many, many books that go through this in minute detail and have well laid out processes and systems to improve your chances. Far too much to cover in one skinny chapter!

What you can takeaway are a few points to help keep you focused and improve your chances of success:

- Never stop learning – your competitors won't, so neither should you;
- Work **on** your business, not in your business. You only have so much time in the day and unless you just want to have a job that pays poorly you need to be working on your business!
- Focus on the customer, the customer and the customer!

We are nearly at the end just one last chapter to wrap it all up!

Is That It? aka Conclusion

"It's not necessary to do extraordinary things to get extraordinary results"

—Warren Buffett

If you have made it this far, you are either one of the cheating readers who jumps to the end of the book to see how it finishes or you have high degree of determination and have actually read all the way to the end! Congratulations – and I should say – thank you.

Let's look at what I hope you have learned along the way:

- A business is more than just a single person selling their own time – it is people, processes and products that can, hopefully, over time grow and be successful.
- Owning and running your own business is genuinely hard work. Don't do it if you don't have the mental strength to put in a huge amount of effort and sustain this over the years. It is very rare to have a successful business that in the beginning can sustain an "easy" time friendly lifestyle! Lifestyle and the "easy" life will come with success but it takes 5+ years to make this happen.
- You don't have to be incredibly talented or a genius to find success in business. You need to understand your strengths and work to them. And work really hard...

- Understand what it is you want to achieve and find a business that fits your objectives and will satisfy what motivates you.
- Owning and running your own business can be very rewarding, in terms of both personal satisfaction and financial outcomes. More people have become truly wealthy through the act of owning their own business than by any other means.
    - o Understand the risks of what you are getting into – Franchise businesses, Business Partnerships – don't leave your job just to find yourself working for someone else!
    - o Have a plan, in place. You may have many plans along the journey – how to leave your job and of course **The** business plan, are just two. Plans don't guarantee success but they certainly improve the probability of success!
    - o Financing and the ability to fund the start of the business or the purchase of the business is very important. You need to get this sorted out and lined up as early as possible and understand what limitations and opportunities you have. Be creative – you will be surprised what you can access in terms of capital.
    - o Finally have the mental courage and motivation to give owning your own business a go…

"In every success story, you will find someone who has made a courageous decision."

—Peter F. Drucker

Bibliography

Anonymous, (2019, April 8) 39 Surprising small business stats for success in 2019. 99 Firms retrieved from https://99firms.com/blog/small-business-statistics/

Anonymous, (2018) 4 Fastest Growing Business Opportunities: New opportunities or Higher Competition. *Next Insurance* retrieved from ***https://www.next-insurance.com/blog/fastest-growing-small-businesses/***

Anonymous, (2019) Number of IPOs in the United States from 1999 to 2018. *Statista* retrieved from ***https://www.statista.com/statistics/270290/number-of-ipos-in-the-us-since-1999/***

Anonymous, (2019) Your Essential Guide to Buying a Small Business, *National Australia Bank NAB* retrieved from ***https://www.nab.com.au/business/moments/starting-out/buy-business/buy-small-business***

Anonymous, (2018, August 14) Business Plan Template and Guide. *Business.gov.au* retrieved from ***https://www.business.gov.au/planning/templates-and-tools/business-plan-template-and-guide***

Barry E (2019 April 4) How to fund the purchase of a small business. *Finder* retrieved from ***https://www.finder.com.au/fund-purchase-of-small-business***

Bhargava R & Herman W (2018) *The Startup Playbook: Founder-to Founder Advice from two Startup Veterans* . Lioncrest Publishing

Campbell A (2018, December 20) Single Person Business Booming. *Small Business Trends* retrieved from https://smallbiztrends.com/2007/07/single-person-businesses-booming.html

Cole N, (2016 August 6) 6 Ways to spot a bad business partner. *Inc.* retrieved from ***https://www.inc.com/nicolas-cole/6-ways-to-spot-a-bad-business-partner.html***

Deibel W(2018) *Buy then Build: How Acquisition Entrepreneurs Outsmart the Startup Game* . Lioncrest Publishing

Draper T(2017) *How to be The Startup Hero.* Independently Published

Gerber, M E (2016) Beyond the *E-Myth – The Evolution of an Enterprise.* Michael E Gerber Companies

Gerber, M E (2004) *The E-Myth Revisted – Why most small businesses don't' work and what to do about it.* Picnic Times

Higgins S, (2018 December 4) The straight forward guide to Target Markets. *Hubspot* retrieved from ***https://blog.hubspot.com/sales/target-market***

Jacob L (2017, February 1) 4 Reasons why a startup product launch can fail. *IQVIS* retrieved from ***https://medium.com/iqvis/4-reasons-why-a-startup-product-launch-can-fail-with-examples-bbd48270f829***

Lisondra G (2019) Borrowing Money to Buy a Business. *mybusiness* retrieved from ***https://www.mybusiness.com.au/sales/3563-borrowing-money-to-buy-a-business***

Lovie K (2017, May 17) Raising finance to buy a business. *Bsale* retrieved from ***https://www.bsale.com.au/blog/raising-finance-to-buy-a-business***

Mansfield M, (2019, March 28) Startup Statistics – The numbers you need to know. *Small Business Trends* retrieved from ***https://smallbiztrends.com/2019/03/startup-statistics-small-business.html***

Robbins T, (2019) Sevens Signs of a Bad Business Partner. *Tony Robbins* retrieved from ***https://www.tonyrobbins.com/business/signs-of-a-bad-business-partner/***

Shewan D, (2019, February 18) 7 of the best value proposition examples we've ever seen. *Wordstream Blog* retrieved from ***https://www.wordstream.com/blog/ws/2016/04/27/value-proposition-examples***

Ward S, (2019 June 2) Simple Business Plan Template. *The balance small business* retrieved from ***https://www.thebalancesmb.com/entrepreneur-simple-business-plan-template-4126711***

Wasserman N (2014) *The Founder's Dilemmas.* Princeton University Press

Young Entrepreneur Council – The, (2017, November 2) 12 Sure signs you shouldn't trust a business partner or vendor. *Small Business Trends* retrieved from ***https://smallbiztrends.com/2015/10/trust-a-business-partner-vendor.html***

Acknowledgements

I would like to acknowledge the Cammeraygal people of the Eora clan, the traditional owners of the land upon which sits my house where I wrote this book. Beyond that I would like to thank Vanessa Kaye and Sandra Peter who very kindly reviewed and critiqued this book before it was released to the public.

It would be unwise of me not to acknowledge my wonderful and supportive family – my wife Ayn (who also helped cast a critical eye over the contents of the book and diligently put an extra space after every full stop…) and Allayne, Phae and Laeph for putting up with me, not only during the writing of this book but also throughout my years of putting my business(es) before my family. In the long run I hope you agree it has all been worth it.

About the Author

I always find it odd talking about myself. So I asked some highly biased and complimentary friends to write a few comments about me:

The Author, Phil is a serial entrepreneur. It all started in primary school, when he set up a business selling tadpoles to private school kids. Soon he was breeding pedigree Himalayan cats and selling the kittens for more than a year's worth of pocket money – each. Before he was 18, he was a manager at the local McDonalds after school. During university, he founded a student association, managed to work and study full time and jagged a job at a pre-IPO Macquarie Bank straight from Uni. In the ensuing years, Phil has started Australia's first peer-to-peer lender, invested in a marina development in Brazil, owned a book store with his wife, bought, grown and (hopefully) exited a multi-million dollar turnover small business, been CTO of an investment bank and become an angel Start-up investor.

When he isn't working on his many ventures, Phil is a married father of 3 children, a soccer team manager, a Sunday morning cyclist and has started collecting rather large koi carp in his fish pond, some of which he manages to keep alive. He hasn't worked out how to make money from them... yet.

Business Owners Boot Camp Checklist

Day #	Weekday	Task	Check
1	Monday	At night redo government required paperwork e.g. tax return	
2	Tuesday	Calculate budget for Baked beans diet Take alternative transport to work	
3	Wednesday	Survive on Baked beans diet	
4	Thursday	Survive on Baked beans diet	
5	Friday	Leave keys/pass at work	
6	Saturday	Go to workplace on weekend (without your keys)	
7	Sunday	Go to workplace on weekend Take home selected documents	
8	Monday	Go to work 1 hour earlier than normal	
9	Tuesday	Go to work 1 hour later than normal	
10	Wednesday	Skip lunch (keep hydrated)	
11	Thursday	Skip lunch (keep hydrated)	
12	Friday	Skip lunch (keep hydrated)	
13	Saturday	Day off!	
14	Sunday	Find documents from Day 7. Place in box and have family member hide them	
15	Monday	Look up the rules on NSW payroll tax and determine via reading case studies, under what conditions an owner driver contractor would make you liable for NSW Payroll tax	

Day #	Weekday	Task	Check
16	Tuesday	Leave work at 7pm (or later) When home trigger circuit breaker and survive without electricity until morning	
17	Wednesday	Find out at your place of work what day of the week the cleaners come to clean the office	
18	Thursday	Leave mobile phone at home	
19	Friday	Skip lunch (keep hydrated)	
20	Saturday	Skip lunch (keep hydrated)	
21	Sunday	Find the hidden documents from Day 14	
		On the day the cleaners clean your office. Work late until the cleaners arrive. No contact with family	
22	Monday	Skip lunch (keep hydrated)	
23	Tuesday	Skip lunch (keep hydrated)	
24	Wednesday	Skip lunch (keep hydrated)	
25	Thursday	Skip lunch (keep hydrated)	
26	Friday	Skip lunch (keep hydrated)	
27	Saturday	Day off	
28	Sunday	Day off	
29	Monday	Family member to set alarm (between midnight – 5am) When alarm goes off go to nearest all night service station and buy a cheap snack	
30	Tuesday	Cut up credit cards put in bin	
31	Wednesday	Take alternative transport to work	

Day #	Weekday	Task	Check
32	Thursday	Cancel credit cards cut up on Day 30	
33	Friday	Leave keys/pass at work	
34	Saturday	Go to workplace on weekend (without your keys)	
35	Sunday	Day off	
		On the day the cleaners clean your office. Work late until the cleaners arrive. With the time update all your new credit card details	
36	Monday	Skip lunch (keep hydrated)	
37	Tuesday	Skip lunch (keep hydrated)	
38	Wednesday	Skip lunch (keep hydrated)	
39	Thursday	Skip lunch (keep hydrated)	
40	Friday	Skip lunch (keep hydrated)	
41	Saturday	Try and walk from home to your work	
42	Sunday	Check your bank account balance. Take note of savings Weigh yourself Take your family out for a meal Finished	

Business Owners Quick Reference Links

Website for searching on businesses for sale (Australia):

AnyBusiness.com.au

Website for setting up a new company:

Cleardocs.com

Website for (free) templates for business plans:

Business.gov.au/planning

Website for easy(?) finance for small businesses:

Prospa.com

Made in United States
North Haven, CT
04 November 2026

21771714R00125